SHELTERED
but NOT
PROTECTED

SHELTERED *but* NOT PROTECTED

Learning to Love, Forgive, and Heal After Emotional and Sexual Abuse

Justin Woodbury

gatekeeper press
Columbus, Ohio

Sheltered but Not Protected: Learning to Love, Forgive, and Heal After Emotional and Sexual Abuse

Published by Gatekeeper Press
2167 Stringtown Rd, Suite 109
Columbus, OH 43123-2989
www.GatekeeperPress.com

Unless otherwise stated, all Scriptures are from *The ESV Study Bible: English Standard Version* (Wheaton, IL: Crossway Bibles, 2007).

The railroad story of Zig Ziglar in chapter 11 was reprinted with permission from Robert Terson, "Zig Ziglar's 'Railroad Story,'" Selling Fearlessly (blog), September 24, 2012, https://www.sellingfearlessly.com/2012/09/24/zig-ziglars-railroad-story/.

The forgiveness article in the author's note was reprinted with permission from Ashley Easter, "What Forgiving an Abuser Doesn't Mean," AshleyEaster.com (blog), February 20, 2017, https://www.ashleyeaster.com/blog/forgiving-doesnt-mean.

Library of Congress Control Number: 2022942634

ISBN (paperback): 9781662929762
eISBN: 9781662930720

Printed in the United States of America

www.shelteredbutnotprotected.com

Dedicated with all my love to my wife, Emily.

There are hundreds of ways to say it—My soulmate. My kindred spirit. My lobster. My one and only. Whatever *it* is, you are *that* for me. Thank you for believing in me, for loving me, for supporting me, for encouraging me. Thank you for being you! I love you, Em.

vi

Contents

But Peter and the apostles answered, "We must obey
God rather than men."

—Acts 5:29

Bad men need nothing more to compass their ends,
than that good men should look on and do nothing.

—John Stuart Mill

Foreword

I waited for him to let me love him.

He was my world, my man, the person I loved deeply with my entire soul, but it didn't matter. I couldn't have him, not yet.

How long? How long would it take to understand, to know, to feel that he was ready to be mine? I didn't know. But I knew that I hated her, what she did to him. What she did to me, to us. How dare she take what was meant to be mine, to be his, ours?

This is a journey that began nine years ago and will continue until death do us part, for that is what I promised. I made a covenant to God, in front of my family, friends, and Jay (my nickname for Justin), that I would honor, love, cherish, forsake all others, and keep myself only to him until death. I was sure that I understood what I was saying, promising. I was sure I knew what love was. And I was sure I knew the God of love. Ours was a fairy-tale story, and it was just beginning. But the next few years proved otherwise as my hopes, dreams, and unrealistic expectations came crashing down around me and left me with a new reality—I needed to learn love. I needed to learn patience. I needed to learn to wait—for him.

* * *

His face was shaking, his body trembling. The man of my dreams had just asked me to marry him. His proposal had exceeded any surprise or present I had ever received. To say I was overjoyed to be his is an understatement! This was the man I had waited for my entire life.

He led me behind a monument on the Fox River Trail to share our first kiss. I wondered why we couldn't just seal the deal right there where he had proposed, but I went along with him, thinking perhaps he was nervous, as was I. But in that most intimate moment, in the promise of forever, the reality of things past creeped in. He leaned in and as we kissed, I realized something was wrong. He was trembling, then he began convulsing. I opened my eyes and was surprised to see that he was staring at me, eyes wide with fear. I quickly pulled away and groaned in my soul as I realized what was haunting this precious moment. "Jay, it's me," I said. "I'm not her. It's okay." He had tears in his eyes as he said, "I know. I'm sorry." I waited for him to feel safe and then we shared a very sweet kiss as the sun set over the Fox River in Aurora, Illinois. We were engaged!

As I share these intimate details of our lives, I do so with no malice or hatred in my heart. I cannot say that I haven't been angry, bitter, or even doubtful of God's love and goodness. I have, more times than I can count. But I share these to show my own ignorance, my pride, my lack of love, and how God gently brought me to a place to begin understanding how much He loves, protects, and selflessly gives mercifully to me daily. And as I continue to understand to learn who He is, to experience His love for me, I am in turn learning to love others as He would have me to.

This journey has been the most challenging of my life because it calls into question everything I have been taught, everything I think I know about God and His Word, my perspective on love, and what it looks like to show it. I'm not a psychologist, nor do I have any experience in counseling, but I know this: I inherited my husband's pain, suffering, experiences, and fears the moment I said "I do." As his wife, his biggest supporter, I was and am determined to learn to do whatever it takes to be the wife he needs me to be, the wife he deserves. One he can trust, confide in, be vulnerable with, and know loves him unconditionally. But unconditional love comes with a cost—and I had no idea just how high.

On September 10, 2011, we became Mr. and Mrs. Woodbury. It was the happiest day of my life. Jay swooped me up in his arms and gently placed me in that limousine, and we were off to our honeymoon. It was perfect, until day three.

I always had ideas and expectations, some intentional, some not. I began questioning why Jay would sometimes pull away when I tried to kiss him, or why he didn't respond when I said or did certain things I assumed would delight him. I moved past the initial disappointment and hurt and thought I just needed to learn him. His love language—yes, that had to be where I was mistaken. But I wasn't.

We settled in a cute little apartment in Littleton, Colorado. If walls could talk, they would have had a volume all on their own. In that little space of 950 square feet, I lost all feeling of hope, love, and security as my promise of "love and cherish" was put to the test, almost daily.

One night shortly after we got married, I waited for Jay to come home. Dinner was ready, and I was wearing a little something-something that was almost nothing-nothing. I was sure he would be pleased. He walked in the door, took one look at me, and said, "Why are you dressed like that?" and continued back into our bedroom to change. I was devastated. I had become vulnerable and tried something new, and this was the response I got? I angrily changed into something more "decent" and thought, "Okay. That doesn't get it done for him, but why not? What's wrong with me? Am I too fat? That must be it. I'll lose weight."

As the evening progressed, thoughts of diets and how quickly they could work consumed me. I passed Jay in the hall and decided I couldn't wait any longer to show him how much I had missed him that day and really wanted him. I said something like, "Hey, baby," and grabbed him by the shoulder. I pushed him up against the wall and started to kiss him deeply. He shoved me away quickly and forcefully and said, wide-eyed, "Why are you doing that? Please don't do that. I don't like that." As he walked away, something inside me died—hope. Hope that this man actually loved me. Did he? How could he and treat me this way? Didn't he want me at all? Why had he married me? Was I to be rejected like this when I tried to show him how much I loved him? Was I unlovable? I hid in the bathroom and sobbed, my heart broken, my confidence in myself, in him, in us gone. This evening was to be the first of many full of uncertainty, sadness, questions, and mostly hurt for both of us as we tried to reach each other.

While I brewed over the next few months over my disappointment in the physical aspect of our married life, I turned to God and His Word. I even met with a pastor's wife and several others for counseling. One woman told me, "God meant you to be with Justin, and I'm sorry to say that this is your life now." Others told me to leave Justin. They said I didn't deserve this kind of life or treatment. Like me, they were convinced that if he truly loved me, he would never put me through this kind of rejection. How was it possible to be so connected in every other aspect but to be so far apart when it came to showing physical love and sharing intimate experiences with each other? Doubt filled my mind daily. Was he cheating on me? Was I ever going to be good enough for him? Skinny enough?

As these thoughts plagued my mind, one truth kept coming back to me like a beacon of light in the darkness: Justin and I were meant to be together. Our story (that is a book in itself) is one full of threads of God, His leading us toward each other. This truth gave me the strength to keep growing, to keep trying to understand my husband. So we continued to share amazing, fun times together, to read each other's thoughts, finish each other's sentences, and share the same hobbies, desires, and even music preferences. I had no doubt that Jay was my man and that God had given him to me. But our physical disconnect was the cause of many arguments, even fights. Oh, how we fought. Jay becoming silent, me slamming doors and screaming at him from the other room that he couldn't possibly love me, promising myself that I would be returning home soon to the people who truly loved me.

I recall during one argument Jay desperately calling out to me as I ran into the bedroom slamming the door, "If you knew how much I loved you, you would be the happiest woman in the world. If you could just see into my heart, you would *know*. You would because I do! I love you so much." But he was right—I couldn't see his heart. And although many of his actions screamed, "I love you," many of them sang a different song that I was interpreting as, "I loathe you."

But somehow, even in those times, I knew we were trying to reach each other. Even when I was certain he was trying to hurt me, I saw pain in his eyes, confusion, and something he couldn't explain or tell me that I so desperately wanted to know and understand. I knew that must be the key, the key that would unlock this wretched box of hurt that was such a big part of our marriage. So I dwelled on all the times Jay had shown me love. They were my bread and butter for years.

And I threw myself into study; I ordered as many books on marriage, love languages, marriage psychology, and sex as I could. I was going to fix this, I thought, even if it meant fixing myself, my perspective on marriage, our reality. And I learned, a lot actually. My communication with Justin improved, as did my ability to show respect. We enjoyed each other; we grew closer. Arguments became a thing of three months' past, then six, then nine, but when they reared their ugly head, those situations escalated quickly and always returned to the familiar theme—rejection, doubt, and insecurity in Jay's love for me.

One night after a moment of physical rejection, I blurted out, "I *hate* what she did to you. I *hate* what it's done to our marriage. I wish so badly you would just get counseling." He looked at me bewildered, and I thought, "How can you possibly *not* know you needed this?" But then I remembered, he had never received counseling. Ever. Had never even been encouraged to pursue that as part of his healing. I considered that maybe we should get counseling together because now *I* needed healing.

The years passed by quickly. Jay never sought counseling, but I continued learning and implementing the ideas as much as I could. My prayer life consisted of thanking God for what "worked," whining about what didn't, and begging Him to heal my heart. I'm not sure exactly when the turning point came, but one evening as we were trying to reach each other physically, I saw fear in his eyes, again. I stopped and began asking questions, just a few. Justin shared a few details I was unaware of before then, and I began to understand. I put myself in his place and realized that he wasn't rejecting me; he was rejecting *her*. He was resisting what *she* had done to him, and I was reminding him of *her*. I wondered what to do and the answer was clear: stop.

What? How could I *not* love on my husband? How could I *not* kiss him? Because he needed me not to. I didn't initiate much more than holding hands after that night because I was waiting for *him*. That was the hardest part of learning and loving my husband, because I wanted him, I needed him—but I couldn't have him.

Then we were blessed with two sweet children. My joy could not be greater. Jackson and Juliette were images of Jay and myself, and they gave us more love, joy, and fullness than we could have imagined. I was comfortable in our new normal; life was busy but full of each other. I had developed a system of carefulness with Justin, showing him affection but not pushing too far, or showing my disappointment when the time between our romp in the hay had become a little greater than I had hoped for. I continued hiding my deep desire to love on my husband in my own way, safely masking it with coping strategies. I still wished that he would love me in the way that I thought I deserved, that made sense to me, that made me feel loved. I began to shut him out of certain thoughts and tempered my sexual feelings to a point that I thought I was emotionally untouchable. I had finally convinced myself that I could no longer be hurt by his distance or our lack of physical intimacy. I had finally learned how to love my husband; I had fixed the "problem," or so I thought.

As I became more passive toward Justin, my journey toward healing began. We had begun attending a new church. As I listened weekly to God's Word being preached, I began to realize that I had no idea who God really was. I had been taught faithfully by my parents about His character, His salvation, and His judgment, but I lacked understanding in one part of His character: His love. Yes, I had sung about it for years. I believed the words of "Jesus Loves Me," and I knew that He "loved" me, but other than hearing about His death for me to save me from God's judgment, myself, and my sins and their consequences (death and eternal separation from God), I didn't know *how* He loved me. I didn't even think of considering this: He *knows* me.

Me! All of me! My thoughts, my frame, how I'm put together, what makes me sad, what makes me happy, what makes me laugh, what makes me cry, what makes me secure, what causes fear in my soul, what makes me who I am. There's no smoke screen, no hiding, He knows it all. And He loves me, all of me, for exactly who He made me to be!

I heard the pastor say emphatically, "You are loved," and realized for the first time that God, the Almighty, my Creator knows all of me and yet somehow not just loves me, He loves me greatly. This beautiful revelation began to stir my heart. I became like a child in a candy store; I needed to learn more of His love. If God could accept me for exactly who I was, how could I learn to accept my husband exactly how he was? And could I attain such a deep level of love that would look past the hurt, bitterness, and everything we had been through and yet help my husband know he was loved for everything he was?

I dug into God's Word and learned how He's patient with me. He doesn't display my sin or talk about it to others. He doesn't strike me down the moment I've sinned. He doesn't point out my flaws or make me a living example of how I "should have done better." He loves me by stating my sin, directly and quietly as I'm listening to His Word being preached at church or as I read it, sometimes in one-word phrases, not shouting or in a lecture. He states it, clearly, concisely. Then, He leaves me alone to consider and to come to Him. He doesn't drag me to Himself or force me to be what I "should be." He waits for me to come to Him, to repent. He waits!

As I started to see this part of my God's character, my life began to change. My anger began to soften; my bitterness slowly became a thing of the past. My heart began to be drawn deeper toward Justin. I loved him even more. My heart ached for him; I was devastated that he couldn't experience physical love without being hurt or afraid or associating it with feeling dirty. My patience and willingness to wait for him grew, and I desperately longed for him to be protected and healed from his past sexual abuse and the horrible aftermath it had caused us. I prayed for healing, for a release from this hold that had been such a cloud over our joys of almost nine years of marriage. I prayed for forgiveness for my own anger and bitterness toward him, his parents, his upbringing, his past cultish church's teachings, his friends who only hurt him more instead of encouraging him to seek help, and the woman at the center of it all. I prayed that I wouldn't wish her dead and that God would give me the ability to pity her as a predator who had taken my husband's innocence without remorse or reservation.

I prayed, I learned, I waited. Then, almost as quickly as the hurt that had so early become a regular visitor in our marriage, it was replaced with something only God can give—peace. Peace in my heart as God answered my prayers, for I had begun praying for what was really His will—harmony in relationships, love, peace, patience, long-suffering, forgiveness, wisdom, growth, gentleness, truth.

Truth! I end that list with truth because it was last on my prayer list. Truth hurts. Truth divides at times. Truth can tear relationships apart, yet I longed for it. I pursued it, howbeit differently than before. I waited for my husband to allow me to love him physically. I waited for my God to show me more of Himself. I waited for God to change my perspective of who I thought He was and how He loved me. I waited to *not* ask the probing questions, I waited to *not* pursue avenues of love that meant so much to me but caused fear in my husband and division in my marriage. I waited.

In 2018, my wait was finally over. Justin began sharing details without my asking of his experience with the woman his mom had called a friend. I listened quietly. I didn't judge. I was careful as my heart wanted to lash out and I wanted this woman put away for good so she couldn't hurt anyone else. I encouraged my husband in truth, in God's love for him. I reminded him that he was a minor when this occurred. I encouraged him to write a book about his experiences. He was hesitant and, at this point of his healing journey, unready to share this incredibly dark, painful part of his life.

But God was working. He is always working! I'm so grateful that He is never done working in us, in our situations, in our hurt, our mistakes, every area of our lives. Justin began forgiving. I could see it. It was evident as he spoke more and more in the following months about how what I did sometimes reminded him of his abusive experience, and we began to communicate as we had needed to in previous years. Our intimacy began to deepen. I learned what was safe for Justin, and he began to feel safer physically with me, more accepted. I didn't demand or request anything except what he was, my man. And what a man he is!

Finally, Justin decided that he needed to share his story. He was experiencing forgiveness and healing as I had never seen before. He was finally at peace. He could talk about Carol Lynn without speaking of her demise. He could talk about sexual abuse without losing his temper. While I was still learning what was safe for him in the bedroom, our intimacy blossomed into that which resembles a glorious honeymoon! Happy days arrived for me in quick succession. Who would have thought the roles would be reversed and so much could be experienced later on in our marriage rather than in the former days? Now if we could only hire a live-in babysitter as we make up for lost time! ☺

One day as Justin was sharing more of his past leading up to the sexual abuse, I said, "It seems as though you were very sheltered but not protected from the sin that envelops every one of us." He looked at me, jumped up from his seat, and exclaimed, "That's it. That's the title of my book! *Sheltered but Not Protected*."

I never would have thought that all the hurt, pain, bitterness, and anger could be transformed into healing of this kind. And I never would have chosen this path for us, nor did I ever consider that from the moment I said "I do" that this is what it meant. It meant that I would begin learning who God really is, not who *I* think He is. It meant that I would begin learning what love really means, learning how to love, learning what it means to be the wife my husband needs, learning how to be someone safe for her husband, learning how to live selflessly, learning how to pray, learning what to pray for, learning to listen, learning to wait, and learning to wait more.

You see, my friend, the answer is . . . *wait*! Loving is waiting. Waiting for the one you love to feel safe with you, waiting for them to share or not share their abusive experience with you, waiting for them to know that their experiences won't be talked about to others by you, waiting for them to understand that they are loved by you by being exactly who they are, understanding that the problem is *not* you and they really do love you but can't show it in ways you wish they would, and that is all right.

So, my friend, wait! Wait for her, for him. I can't promise that you won't hate parts of the journey, the struggles as you desperately try to reach that person. But if you love them with everything you are, you'll realize as I did that in loving them, you are part of their healing, their comfort, their joy as they walk through their past, present, and future with you as their biggest supporter. Support is patience, patience is selfless, selfless is giving up every expectation, every demand, and the let-me-fix-you notion as you wait. *You can't fix them!* Wait for them to heal, to feel safe with you, to have those most intimate moments without associating you with their past experiences, fears, and hurt.

So as you wait, love. Love them with your whole being however they feel loved, expecting nothing in return. As you learn their needs in different circumstances or settings, you will begin to understand their hurt, their suffering, and their fears, and those will become yours. So bear all these along with them because they need you to.

As I walk through this journey with Justin, I'm beginning to understand what the phrase "God is love" really means. "Love is patient and kind; love does not envy or boast; it is not arrogant or rude. It does not insist on its own way; it is not irritable or resentful; it does not rejoice at wrongdoing, but rejoices with the truth. Love bears all things, believes all things, hopes all things, endures all things" (1 Corinthians 13:4–7). God loves us all in these ways, and I will continue striving till my dying day to love my husband, too.

As you read my husband's account of his sexual abuse and how God brought him to healing and forgiveness, I hope you will find peace, love, forgiveness, healing, and encouragement, whether you have been abused, know someone who was, or are even married to a victim of abuse. And if you're the one waiting, there is hope. It may take time, a lifetime, perhaps. But he or she is worth it. Please, wait!

Emily Woodbury
July 2020

Chapter 1—The Beginning

I had the best childhood. My father, a high school dropout, had climbed his way up the corporate ladder at an international airline company until he became the vice president of operations. He is a hard worker, a great father, and one of my closest friends—something I've found to be rare between fathers and sons. After having gone through a bitter divorce and losing his first family, he lovingly spoiled my sister and me, and he lived to make sure we were happy and fulfilled.

Because my dad made more than enough money, my mother was able to stay at home. Mom didn't take that responsibility lightly. She was an amazing cook, kept our house clean, and always made sure we had clean laundry. She also loved having fun and going on adventures with us. For example, almost every day one summer, Mom would take us to the park or to a friend's or nearby lake to swim after teaching us how. She was laid-back, patient, and selfless with her time. She loved my sister and me deeply, and I've never doubted her love for us.

Mom could have had ten children and been a great mother, but because of how hard pregnancy was for her, my parents decided to stop at just me and my older sister, Shannon. Shannon and I are two years apart to the day. We were very close growing up and played together every day until we became teens. Even though we had different interests and hobbies, we always found a way to compromise. My G.I. Joes would ride on the back of her My Little Ponies, or we would play Little House on the Prairie—she would be all the girl characters and I would just be Pa. Shannon was best friends with a family in our church with seventeen sisters and cousins, so there were a lot of girls at our house all the time. I was accepted by Shannon and her girlfriends and have fond memories growing up with them.

We lived on a small semiworking farm, where we raised pigs, chickens, and turkeys until Dad's work schedule got too crazy and we had to get rid of the animals. We had no neighbors; the closest house was separated by hundreds of acres of cornfields. In the summertime after eating breakfast, Shannon and I would disappear in the cornfields for hours, sometimes only breaking to devour the many fruits and vegetables in our garden. Then we would go back off into the cornfields exploring. When I was around eight years old, my parents bought us a horse named Tazaratha and a dirt bike. Shannon and I would ride Taz for hours on end, playing cowboys or Little House on the Prairie. When we got bored or when Shannon didn't want to play anymore, I would strip down to my underwear and remove the reins and saddle from Taz to play Indians, running her bareback through the fields and hollering at the top of my lungs. When that got boring, I got dressed and jumped on my dirt bike, tearing up and down the fields until I ran out of gas.

Shortly after buying our farm, Dad invested in a 1959 John Deere 630 tractor. I learned to drive that John Deere when I was four, and some of my fondest memories were on that tractor. During the winter months, Dad made little jumps in the snow out in the fields. Our friends would come over with their sleds and we would tie them all together in a line, sometimes five or six in a row, and attach them to the tractor. Dad drove around the fields and over the jumps on the John Deere. Inevitably someone always fell off and would have to wait for the tractor to come back around to get on. Once in a while someone in the front would fall off and not be able to move out of the way quick enough, so they would hit the sled behind them and that pile would hit the sled behind them until the entire group of eight to ten kids were all piled on top of each other, laughing uncontrollably. When we got too cold to stay outside, we would all go inside around the woodburning stove and thaw out while enjoying cups of hot cocoa.

Family vacations were the best. Every year for several years, we rented a cabin right on a river that led to Lake Michigan. This is where I fell in love with water. I spent every moment I could snorkeling in that river or swimming in Lake Michigan. When I wasn't swimming, Shannon and I went fishing, or our family would take a boat ride down the river to Lake Michigan. Sometimes we climbed the sand dunes in the area. Sometimes at night we had a bonfire on Lake Michigan and roasted hot dogs and marshmallows. Other times we went to the ice cream parlor next to our cabin and sat on the river eating our ice cream. We cherished our time at that cabin. Eventually the rent for just one day became more than for the week when we first started renting it, so we began vacationing in other places, states, and even countries. When Shannon and I stopped attending a Christian school and began homeschooling, we had a lot of opportunities to travel and do other things throughout the school year, too.

My parents brought us up in church faithfully. I was there every Sunday morning, Sunday evening, Wednesday evening, Thursday evening for visitation (what we called going door-to-door passing out gospel tracts or following up with first-time visitors), and most Saturdays for men's prayer meeting. I can recall only a few times I missed church if we were in town. When we went on vacation, we faithfully attended another Baptist church in the area.

As a child and into my early teens, I loved attending our church. There was an excitement about serving Jesus that was attractive and contagious. Because our church was so small, everybody knew everybody, and friendships were forged that

have withstood the test of time. Our pastor and founder—
Preacher, as we called him—was like a second father to me. He
was one of the hardest-working men I've ever known, and he
was always working on a project, either at the church or at his
house. Growing up I spent many afternoons helping him with
his different construction projects. He taught me a lot about
building, landscaping, plumbing, and more, and for that I am
forever grateful. The assistant pastor, Pastor B, was also a great
father figure and one of the most generous men I've ever known.
I'll never forget complimenting him on his watch when I was six
or seven and him taking it off and giving it to me.

Our church was made up of all first-generation Christians,
meaning every founding member didn't come to know Christ
until they were adults. Each member including Preacher had
been a Christian for only a few years, so every one of them had
experienced life without Christ and what it had to offer—or
rather not offer. I sincerely believe that from the staff down to the
congregation, each member wanted something different for the
next generation. They didn't want their children to experience
the same empty and sometimes tragic situations they had lived
through. But instead of channeling their desire in a healthy way,
they created an environment so sheltered that it led to its own
set of tragedies.

Chapter 2—Sheltered

To help shelter the next generation from a life without Christ, the church established certain rules and regulations. These were not initiated overnight but rather took place over more than thirty years. We were taught that these rules were God's rules and that each one of them came directly from the Bible. I can't remember the specific order that these rules were adopted in, just that they were part of my life growing up and were mandated through our church as part of a lifestyle we should be living. In the early years, I believe the leadership's desire for holiness and godliness was the driving force behind these rules. Gradually, however, manipulation and control began replacing their initial intentions.

One of our congregation's biggest restrictions was with music. We were never allowed to listen to any "worldly" music unless it was classical. Drums, guitars, handheld mics, and anything related to rock music was believed to be straight from the pits of hell. I'd sit through several messages at church trying to figure out what the speaker meant when he compared the way a woman "sensually handled" a microphone to something that God intended only for marriage. We sang hymns from only the nineteenth and twentieth centuries in church as well as in our house. We were taught that because the heart beats with a rhythm of *pum*-pum, *pum*-pum—with emphasis on beats one and three—that the beat in music should follow the same pattern. Therefore, any music that followed the pattern of pum-*pum*, pum-*pum*, the beat of most rock songs, was worldly and from the devil. This beat, they argued, caused the body to move in a sensual way, also known as dancing, which was strictly forbidden, too, even between married couples. In my teen years my friends and I used to quietly joke, "Don't ever have sex; it could lead to dancing."

Until we were much older, we didn't really watch movies or TV, except *Little House on the Prairie*, the occasional *Wonderful World of Disney*, and the *Bugs Bunny & Tweety Show*. We were one of the only families in our church who owned a TV. We always shut off the commercials, muted any scenes that had the "rock beat," and switched channels anytime there was a hand-holding or kissing scene. When *Honey, I Shrunk the Kids* came out on VHS, we weren't allowed to watch it because we were told there was a sex scene. Once when I was staying at a friend's house, I was allowed to pick a movie and chose *Honey, I Shrunk the Kids*. I was pretty surprised to find that the "sex scene" was just an on-screen kiss.

As we became older and foul-language filtering devices such as TVGuardian came on the market, we were allowed to watch other movies. Sometimes when a woman with a short or low-cut dress came on screen, one of my sister's friends would hold a pillow over whichever half revealed the most. If you're picturing a nine-year-old boy wondering what was behind that pillow, you're wrong—I was in my late teens and early twenties.

Going to the movie theater, regardless of the movie, was strictly forbidden because it was considered an easy setting for bad things to happen. Going to Blockbuster Video was frowned upon but generally overlooked.

Our rules didn't stop with media. Even our clothing was strictly regulated with the intention of preventing lust as well as the patriarchal desire to control women and ultimately blame them for sexual situations such as rape and sexual abuse. In the church's beginning, it was simple—women wore dresses and men wore pants. This wardrobe conviction was taken so seriously that someone at church went through the children's books and drew dresses and higher tops on the women, pants on the men wearing shorts, and clothes on any naked animal characters. I sincerely used to feel sad when I'd see a woman in pants because I believed she was probably going to hell. It wasn't until my late teens that I began to question my thinking on this.

"If it's long enough and full enough, you can do whatever you need to do," Preacher would say, referring to why women couldn't wear pants for any activity—whether skiing, horseback riding, or visiting theme parks. "If an activity doesn't allow you to wear a dress and still be modest, then you don't need to participate." What Preacher didn't realize is that these safeguards didn't fully protect a woman's modesty—or turn off our adolescent hormones. I saw a lot of legs and panties from women wearing long and full skirts. But I never saw up a woman's pants.

What we wore had very little room for leeway, but there were no gray areas when it came to alcohol. We were taught that any negative reference to wine or alcohol in the Bible was referring to actual alcohol, while any positive reference to wine or alcohol in the Bible was referring to grape juice. Jesus did not consume one drop of alcohol and warned against one drop of alcohol, and therefore it had no place in a Christian's life.

Many of these rules were intended to keep us pure, especially the younger generation. This extreme quest for purity was why our church also considered dating wicked. Dating led to sex, which led to dancing. Instead of dating, we believed in courtship. In the earlier years of the church, my generation was taught that courtship was just parental-supervised dating for the sole purpose of marriage. As we got older, this morphed into a concept known in our circles as faith-based mate finding (FBMF).

Here's what a typical FBMF scenario looked like: The father of an eligible son would approach the father of an eligible daughter and discuss the possibility of a union between their children. This was then discussed and prayed about between the four parents. If the parents concluded that the Lord willed this relationship, the children were brought into the decision and were given anywhere from a few weeks to a few months to pray about it. They were allowed to visit each other during this time, but these meetings were always supervised.

Once the children agreed with their parents' decision (which was more often than not), they became engaged and married as soon as possible, regardless of their age. During the engagement, visits and conversations still had to be supervised or chaperoned. Some parents even listened in on the phone calls between the couple. There was zero physical contact until the wedding night—no hand-holding, no hugging, no nothing. The couple was supposed to follow the six-inch rule, meaning that at any time, there had to be at least six inches between them. When church members saw Shannon's engagement pictures showing her now husband holding her hand up to get a good shot of her ring, they lost their minds!

Eventually, Preacher introduced another concept called mental, emotional, and physical impurity that provided even more specific guidelines regarding purity:

- **Mental impurity**—thinking about anyone of the opposite sex in any way other than that of an appropriate brother-sister relationship
- **Emotional impurity**—being emotionally attracted to or having romantic feelings toward anyone of the opposite sex that you aren't courting or engaged to

- **Physical impurity**—any physical contact with someone of the opposite sex unless it is a family member

Many of us ended up attending a very conservative university that shared a similar philosophy on sexual purity. I remember sitting in a men's chapel session at college discussing what was appropriate regarding men and women touching each other—should you shake hands with a woman? Hug her? One particular freshman was listening intently as he took everything in, a look of sheer agony on his face. Finally, he raised his hand and in a trembling voice said, "Let's pretend I am walking down the stairs at church when all of a sudden, I hear a commotion behind me. When I turn around, there is a woman who has tripped and is falling down the stairs toward me. I can either reach out my hand and stop her from falling down the rest of the stairs, or I can step aside so as not to touch her and let her continue to fall. What should I do?" I laughed out loud because I thought it was so funny, but the rest of the men talked it out as if it were a real question.

FBMF was supposed to be completely faith based, meaning feeling wasn't supposed to be involved. This omission was tragic because I had friends get engaged and within weeks of their marriage admit that they didn't love or even like their fiancée, but by faith they knew it was the Lord's will.

In addition, the no-touch policy as well as the chaperone requirement often yielded many negative results. In many cases, the couple followed those rules without compromise. Couples went from never being alone and never touching to being pressured to consummate their marriage overnight. This led to major issues on their wedding night, with consummation taking days and sometimes weeks. I've had many college friends confide in me that following those strict guidelines almost ruined their marriage.

In other cases, the couple simply pretended to follow the rules. For engaged couples at our church, the ultimate proclamation at the marriage altar was that they didn't kiss or even hold hands until the day of their wedding. Many couples who didn't follow the six-inch rule were still able to claim this because they just ran right from home plate to third base. I knew many couples who never kissed, held hands, or had sex but did everything else you can imagine. This caused so much regret and mistrust between the spouses, and many issues in their marriage that some are still dealing with even after several years.

Another problem FBMF caused was actually the opposite of jumping into a marriage that shouldn't happen. If a parent or sibling disagreed with a union, it was off—regardless of the child's age. I could write a separate book about regretful "children" in their thirties, forties, and sometimes even fifties who were interested in somebody but didn't pursue marriage because at least one parent didn't think it was the Lord's will.

Don't get me wrong—I'm not against rules and safeguards, and I don't let my children watch anything or do anything they want. I'm against imbalance—like these extreme regulations created—and the devastating effects growing up in an imbalanced environment can cause.

As our church continued to grow, so did the extreme rules, and so did the lack of a relationship with God among the members. It was easy to wear a suit and tie or a long, full dress and declare "Thus sayeth the Lord" on Sunday and then live the way you wanted the rest of the week. And as long as someone talked the talk, it was assumed they walked the walk. As a result, our church became a breeding ground for weird, twisted, and perverted people and situations. Abuse in all forms—sexual, physical, and psychological—was not only tolerated but in some cases encouraged. I would come to experience this perversion firsthand when I was seventeen.

Chapter 3—Kathy, Bill, and Rashawn

As early as I can remember and into my teen years, our family would leave for choir practice every Sunday afternoon at four o'clock and stay for the evening service. While my mom was practicing, my dad, one of the wisest men I know, used to sit in the back of the auditorium and tell me and my friends stories about when he was growing up, earning him the affectionate nickname Uncle Woody.

Sometimes, though, he would take me aside and teach me life lessons. One lesson that burned itself into my memory was to watch for wolves in sheep's clothing. Three different times he pointed to three different people and said, "Justin, mark my words—those people are into something bad, and they're acting that way to cover it up." What he meant by "that way" was taking the church's already rigid standards to the extreme to give the appearance of being godly. Even though it took months, even years sometimes, for the "something bad" to come out, my dad was never wrong. Here are the stories of those three people.

Kathy

I don't remember a time not knowing John, Preacher's brother. At one point he wasn't allowed to come to our church because he was under church discipline for marrying Kathy, who left her husband for him. John seemed to be knowledgeable about many things and could carry on conversations for hours, especially with women. When John and Kathy were finally let back into church, our family invited their family over for dinner. That's when we began to really get to know Kathy.

Kathy, who was several years younger than John, took the already extreme modest dress standards to the extreme. While most men in our church didn't wear shorts, Kathy wouldn't allow her husband to wear shorts or even short sleeves. And while other women wore long, full dresses and blouses, Kathy and her daughters wore bloomers underneath their dresses and sweaters over their blouses. If someone in the church didn't dress to their standard, Kathy, or her young kids would confront them. I'll never forget the day my nanna came back from a church function bewildered because one of Kathy's children confronted her about her low top.

Everyone in the church seemed to know about Kathy's bizarre standards, but nothing was ever done about it. Her holier-than-thou attitude continued for several years, and one day, Kathy left John for another man in our church named Jim. Jim was married and in his seventies—a good forty years older than Kathy. He and his wife, Nachee, attended our church semiregularly. What I remember most about Jim is that after service he always had a group of children around because he passed out candy. I was too young to remember all the details of why Kathy left John, but I know it had to do with John not providing for his family.

The affair between Jim and Kathy didn't last long. When Kathy got all that she could get from Jim, she made his life a living hell, stalking him, calling his house, and, if the rumors were true, ramming her car into his after he left his house one day. I saw Kathy only once after the affair went south when she was picking up her kids at church.

I was ten or eleven when my dad warned me about Kathy's extremes and other church members who acted as if they had attained a level of spirituality far above his spiritual contemporaries. It wasn't long after that when my dad pointed out Bill.

Bill

Bill visited our church for the first time when I was around twelve years old. He was tall and thin with long hair and was in a rock band. He made a profession of faith a few months later and began to attend church regularly. Every few months Bill would be "convicted" about his long hair and get a haircut. Each time he would get a few more inches cut until eventually his hair—as he was supposedly told—was the way God would have it: above the ears with a comb-over.

Shortly after becoming a Christian, Bill enrolled in a local Bible college. On Sunday evenings when the choir practiced on stage in the auditorium, Bill could often be found in the front row reading his Bible. Sometimes after church he would find a high-traffic area and study his Bible there. Eventually Bill became combative about spiritual issues and started confronting people about their walk with the Lord. He was judgmental, condescending, and proud.

One day at a men's prayer meeting, Bill asked my dad how he was doing. When Dad responded with, "Good, Bill. How are you?" Bill retorted, "Stan, the Bible says there is none good but One." I'll never forget my dad's response. He looked Bill in the eye and said, "Bill, when you die, they're going to give you an enema and bury you in a matchbox." Later that night, my dad told me to keep an eye out for Bill because no doubt, he was hiding something.

A few months later, Bill didn't show up at church on Sunday, then on Wednesday or Thursday. He wasn't at men's prayer meeting on Saturday or in church the next Sunday either. In total, Bill was absent from church for over a month. When he returned, he had a mustache and a much humbler demeanor. He had been courting a woman in our church during that time, but the relationship didn't last. Not long after he came back, a few of us saw them in a heated argument outside after church. It was pretty clear she was breaking up with him.

Bill began spending many nights in Preacher's office with Preacher and the deacons. A few weeks after Bill's return, Preacher announced one Sunday night after service that we were going to have a church-family meeting. Preacher started the meeting by telling everyone that the reason Bill hadn't been in church was because he'd been in jail. He then invited Bill up to the front to read his letter of apology for sinning against God as well as the church body. The letter was so vague that by the time he was finished reading it, none of us knew anything more than that Bill was sorry. Preacher then dismissed everyone under eighteen, which included me, so Bill could share the details of his great sin with the adult members—a very effective shaming technique that I was to experience years later.

A few months after that meeting, Dad told me what had happened. When Bill was a young kid, he thought it was fun to streak around the house naked to get a reaction out of his family. They thought it was a cute stage he would grow out of, but he didn't. When Bill was in his twenties, he began publicly exposing himself to random women and then going home to masturbate to their reaction.

One day, Bill was watching people through the peephole of his apartment door, naked. When a particular woman walked by, he opened the door to get the morning newspaper and in doing so exposed himself. The woman reported Bill to the police, which landed him in jail. After his short time in jail, Bill continued to regularly attend our church but wasn't able to deal with his problem. He needed professional help, but he was only offered counseling from one of the men in our church. Eventually Bill moved to another state. Sadly, the last I had heard of him was that he had parked his car about a mile from a local mall, stripped down naked, and ran as far as he could until he was arrested and put back in jail. The judge told him that since he was a repeat offender, he had one more strike before they put him away for life.

Rashawn

Kathy and Bill weren't the only extremist church members whose sexual issues were brought to light. Rashawn, her sister, and a few of their friends began attending our church during my teen years. Rashawn was single and wore long, full dresses, just like what was expected of any woman in our church. However, she had another conviction that our church didn't hold—head coverings. Rashawn believed that according to 1 Corinthians 11, a woman ought not enter into a church sanctuary without something on her head. Usually that something was a doily or piece of cloth, although one time I did see one of Rashawn's friends grab a tissue out of desperation and place it on her head before she walked into the auditorium. My friends and I assumed it was because she couldn't find anything else to wear.

Like Bill, Rashawn also sat in the very front of the auditorium during choir practice and read her Bible there before the evening church service. And like both Kathy and Bill, she also seemed to possess a superior relationship with God.

When I was in my late teens, Rashawn began meeting regularly with Preacher and his wife, Joy. Eventually, she stopped coming to church, and it was rumored that another church discipline meeting was about to happen. Sure enough, a few weeks later after service, Preacher announced an "after meeting." The rumors were true; Rashawn was being church disciplined. Her sin? She was a nymphomaniac, and she was not willing or able to stop her behavior. Preacher warned each of us, including Rashawn's sister, Pam, that part of church discipline in this case meant we were to have no contact with Rashawn until she was repentant. Pam took this advice to heart and had nothing to do with Rashawn for years. I was told that Pam and her kids even left in the middle of a Thanksgiving family dinner because Rashawn showed up.

Although these three situations were some of the most extreme, similar ones happened every few years. My heart goes out to those people who should have received professional counseling and help but were only chastened and shunned. I've also grown to realize that in many of these situations, the church was guilty of overreaching, and should have not gotten involved.

In my teens I learned pretty quickly to avoid the extremists at our already extreme church. That's why I loved spending time with the Mathia family. They seemed so normal and down to earth. I soon found out in the worst way possible that this was far from true through one phone call that changed the entire course of my life.

Chapter 4—Mrs. Mathia

In the spring of 1998, I was a junior in high school and couldn't wait for summer. My best friend, Noah, and I were starting our own lawn mowing and landscaping business—Cutting Edge Lawn and Landscapes. Noah had already been mowing lawns around his neighborhood for the past couple of years, but we had recently purchased everything we needed to officially begin our business: three walk-behind lawnmowers, a Weedwacker, a blower, an edger, and a fourteen-foot trailer to pull it all in. We stored the equipment in my family's barn, anticipating all the fun we would have working together.

One day that spring while I was doing schoolwork, the phone rang. Since Mom was out running an errand, I picked it up. It was Mrs. Mathia.

The Mathias were close family friends and trusted members of our church. Before they joined our congregation, Preacher had been warned about them by the pastor of their previous church, but the details were blurry, so we welcomed them with open arms. Before long, they were an intricate part of the ministry, involving themselves and their kids in almost every outreach our church offered.

Mr. and Mrs. Mathia were in their midthirties. Mr. Mathia was tall and skinny with a mustache and a good sense of humor. I enjoyed when our families got together because he could always make me laugh. Mrs. Mathia had a great sense of humor as well. She wore long, modest dresses and jumpers (known as frumpers among the teen girls who hated jumpers), sang in the choir, played in the orchestra, and worked in the nursery. She was always nice and seemed to love God and her husband. She went forward during the altar call on many occasions, crying over something she was convicted about during the message. And although most adults in our church didn't interact much with children, Mrs. Mathia always made me feel special.

When I started going through puberty as a teen, I became very insecure. It seemed like I grew three inches and two waist sizes overnight, which made all my pants look like tight capris. My voice was changing, I was growing facial hair—and I began noticing women in a completely different light. It was during this time that Mrs. Mathia began to take an interest in me. Abusers often groom their victims for years before abusing them, so at the time, her attention seemed harmless to me and apparently most everyone else. Everything Mrs. Mathia did during my early teen years was in plain sight. She sought me out at church functions and talked to me about things that would interest a thirteen-year-old boy—usually sports, working out, and motorcycles. Mrs. Mathia also talked to me about spiritual matters, often encouraging me to obey my parents and pursue God with all my heart.

I enjoyed our talks and often poured my heart out to Mrs. Mathia about things weighing heavy on me. She was like a second mother to me; she listened and cared. Sometimes she would even defend me to my dad if I got in trouble with another adult at church. I trusted her completely, and so did my parents. I only learned many years later that a couple at church had pleaded with Preacher and other men to keep a watchful eye on Mrs. Mathia's relationship with me as it seemed unnatural. Their pleading was ignored.

When I turned fifteen, my growth spurt slowed long enough for my mom to buy pants that actually fit me. I began lifting weights and running, and I grew proportionately into my body. That year Shannon graduated from high school, and she and her best friend celebrated with a joint open house in our barn. We spent days cleaning it out in preparation, including moving all my workout equipment out of sight behind a wall with a trap door that opened into the barn's nursery, where we used to keep our pigs.

On the day of the event, I was hanging out with my friends when the Mathias showed up. During the course of the evening, Mrs. Mathia came over to say hi and we sat down and started talking. At one point she asked, "Isn't this where you lift weights?" referring to the section of the barn we were in. I told her yes but that we had moved everything over for the party. Then she asked me if I could show her where we moved them, so I led her to the equipment. She asked if I could teach her how to bench-press, and I agreed.

As she lay down on the bench press machine and lifted the weights off the rack, I grabbed the barbell from behind the bench to spot her, just like I had for friends so many times before. I made sure my hands were close enough to the outside of the barbell to avoid making any contact with her body. But somehow, as Mrs. Mathia brought the weights down, my right hand was suddenly directly on top of her right breast. I quickly picked the barbell back up, placed it on the bench rest, and tried my best to pretend that nothing had happened. I had never kissed a girl or even held a girl's hand, much less touched a woman's breast. There was no doubt in my mind that this had been an accident. I knew Mrs. Mathia; she was an adult, and she would never be inappropriate.

Over the next two years, I continued speaking with Mrs. Mathia and confiding in her. It never occurred to me that any interaction with her could have been less than innocent. So when the phone rang that day and Mrs. Mathia was on the other line, nothing was different.

When I answered the phone, Mrs. Mathia asked to speak to my mom. I told her that Mom was out running errands and to call back in a few hours. Just as I was hanging up, she said, "Wait, I have to tell you something. The other night I had a dream about you."

"Really?" I asked, curious. "What was it about?"

At first, Mrs. Mathia teased me by sharing only bits and pieces, but I knew she wasn't telling me everything. Finally, after very little prodding, she told me she had dreamed that we had gotten married. "You were the best sex I had ever had," she said. As a seventeen-year-old who had so many questions but very few answers, I was intrigued. We talked for over an hour that day. That's when Mrs. Mathia admitted that she had started becoming attracted to me when I turned thirteen, and that her attraction had only grown.

I sat there on the couch with our cordless phone, feeling things I had never felt before. My heart was pounding; my palms were sweaty. I was nervous and confused, but also excited. I couldn't believe that a woman was attracted to me, and even though she was older and married, I was flattered. We had always been taught that it was wrong to like girls, but for some reason this seemed okay because she was married and old enough to be my mother.

Eventually my mom returned from shopping, and we hung up. During Wednesday service that evening, every time I looked over in the Mathias's direction, Mrs. Mathia was staring at me, the most sensual look on her face. I don't think she broke her gaze from me the entire service. After church, when we passed in a crowded hall, she purposely rubbed her body up against mine.

That weekend the entire Mathia family stopped by our house unexpectedly. We were all standing in the kitchen talking when Mrs. Mathia positioned herself behind me in the doorway leading into our hall. Suddenly I felt her hand on the small of my back, moving slowly down until she was rubbing my butt. I froze, not knowing what to do.

During that next week, Mrs. Mathia and I talked almost every day, sometimes for hours at a time. She now wanted me to call her by her first name, Carol Lynn, which felt awkward at first, but I obliged. Our conversations were mostly sexual, and Carol Lynn seemed to know a lot about sex and the human anatomy. She told me about her body and asked me about mine. She asked if I ever masturbated and thought about her. She also told me that when she was having sex with Fred—Mr. Mathia— she had to bury her face in a pillow to keep from moaning my name.

One day that week, Carol Lynn stopped by to pick apples from our tree. When she was done, she came inside for a bit. Although we had company over, Carol Lynn asked me right in front of our guests if she could see my room. I took her upstairs, and once we were inside, she grabbed me and began french-kissing me, sticking her tongue so far down my throat I almost gagged. It was an experience I wasn't ready for. I pushed her away and muttered, "Please stop," and we went downstairs to rejoin my family's guests. When Carol Lynn was ready to leave, she asked me to help her out to the van with the apples she'd picked. Once we were out of sight behind her van, she kissed me again.

That night in bed, I felt gross. I had always dreamed about my first kiss and what it would feel like. I thought it would be sweet and gentle and soft, not rough and definitely not with tongue.

Carol Lynn and I continued to talk on the phone into the summer. Because the mowing business had started, I now had a cell phone and a pager. Carol Lynn had both numbers, but she usually paged me with a made-up phone number when she wanted to talk but didn't want her number to show up on my caller ID. Part of her fake phone number—which intentionally contained "69"—was the same as the hymn number to "Day by Day," so she called the hymn "our song" because she wanted to be with me "day by day, and with each passing moment."

A week after my first kiss, Mom told us that Mrs. Mathia and her kids would be coming over because she needed some time to de-stress in an environment away from their home. Carol Lynn had confided in my mom just a few days earlier that she was "going through some things" and needed a friend. Mom was close to Carol Lynn, so she welcomed the opportunity to help a friend.

The night before Carol Lynn and her kids came over, one of the teens in our youth group passed away suddenly from a medical condition. When my mom shared the news with Carol Lynn and her kids at our house the next day, Carol Lynn broke down, sobbing uncontrollably as she sat down at our kitchen table. While she was regaining her composure, the Mathia kids asked me if they could play in our barn. When I came back inside from letting them into the barn, Carol Lynn was still in tears. Not wanting to be around crying women, I decided to go back out to check on the kids.

As I was walking out the door, Carol Lynn caught up with me and told me she wanted to make sure her kids were safe. The moment we were out of sight inside the barn, it happened again. Carol Lynn grabbed me and we began kissing. Suddenly she stopped and said, "I want you to look into my eyes while we are kissing." So I did.

I can't completely explain the feeling of staring into her eyes as we kissed. But it was unnatural, and I hated every second of it. Even though her children were right above us and anyone could have walked into the barn, we did a lot more than kissing that day. I experienced a lot of firsts, but kissing Carol Lynn with my eyes open stood out most because it made me feel dirty. It wasn't until years later that I read articles that linked kissing with your eyes open to psychopathic behavior.

That weekend people came from all over the state to attend the funeral for the teen in our youth group. Preacher's niece, whom I hadn't seen for years, was there, and we got to talking. She was my age and had turned into a beautiful young woman. There seemed to be some chemistry between us, and as we finished our conversation, she wrote her number on a piece of paper and handed it to me. When I turned around to leave our conversation, I saw Carol Lynn across the auditorium glaring at me.

After the funeral, she approached me. "What did that girl give you?" she asked.

"Her phone number," I responded.

"May I see it?" she said.

When I handed Carol Lynn the scrap of paper, she crinkled it up and put it in her mouth. "If you're with me," she said with her mouth full of paper, "you aren't going to be with any other woman."

But you're married, I thought, confused by her logic. Because I was inexperienced with relationships, though, I went along with it, regardless of her strange reaction.

Over the next several months, I became caught up in the most twisted sexual relationship with Carol Lynn. I continued to experience many firsts, and even some lasts, with her. We

talked on the phone almost daily about everything sexual—
with many calls dominated by me asking questions to clarify
something she was talking about. Often in the middle of our
dirtiest conversations, she would challenge me spiritually or tell
me she was praying for me, and then go right back into the dirty
talk.

She continued to stare at me lustfully during church
and rubbing herself up against me anytime the opportunity
presented itself. One Friday night during a reception for a music
recital the church hosted, Carol Lynn asked me and my friend
Susan if we wanted to take a walk with her down to the woods.
Susan hesitated but agreed, and we began making our way
down the sidewalk toward the woods. It was dark out, and as we
began getting closer to the woods and further from the parking
lot lights, Carol Lynn began acting giddy and strange. I started
getting very nervous. I had no idea what she had planned, but
it all seemed too weird. At that moment I heard, "Justin! Get
back here!" It was my dad, and he sounded furious. We all
immediately turned around and walked back into church.

That night at home, my dad called a family meeting. "Stay
away from Carol Lynn," he demanded. "She is sick, and I don't
like the way she acts around you. I think she's just looking for a
hard body. Also, Fred doesn't seem all that stable, and he's liable
to come after you if he sees the way his wife is sniffing around
you."

"Stan!" my mom blurted out. "You are so perverted. Carol
Lynn is my friend, and I don't appreciate you accusing her like
this." I promised both of my parents that nothing was going
on and asked to be excused. I immediately went to my room,
trembling and confused. I wanted so badly to tell my dad
everything that had been going on, but I was terrified. I knew
all too well the punishment and shame that would await me if

our church found out what happened. Besides, Carol Lynn had convinced me that what we were doing was somehow okay, and I trusted her. Thanks to my dad's warnings, that night was the turning point in my bizarre and twisted relationship with Carol Lynn.

My dad's suspicions didn't stop me from calling Carol Lynn, which I usually did between lawn jobs because my parents couldn't overhear me. I don't remember all the conversations, but I do remember when they got very, very bizarre. We were in the middle of talking about something when all of a sudden, she began crying. "What's wrong?" I asked her.

Sobbing, she said, "I want to see you grow up and serve God, but I can't stand the thought of you getting married to anyone but me. On the day of your wedding, I will be sitting in the congregation heartbroken, knowing it should have been me." She paused. "If we could just figure out a way to get married. My kids adore you, and I think over time they would think of you as their father. Can't you just hear them calling you 'Daddy'?"

No, I can't, I thought.

"The only problem is that if we continued attending our church as a married couple and as a family, I couldn't just divorce Fred," she said, referring to our church's strict divorce and remarriage policy. "No, we would have to figure something else out . . . Hey, what was that poison in your coffee recipe you were telling me about?"

I almost dropped the phone. She was referring to a recipe I had read in *The Anarchist Cookbook*, which I had recently downloaded from a floppy disk a friend had given me. I had no idea of the full contents of this book, only that it contained recipes for bombs I could build and detonate under some stumps we were trying to get rid of on the farm. However, the particular recipe she mentioned involved extracting nicotine from tobacco and putting it in someone's coffee. Allegedly it was tasteless, untraceable, and almost instantly lethal. After my initial shock, I quickly steered the conversation elsewhere.

At that point in our "relationship," I began looking for ways out. I'd started out as a curious teen following the lead of a trusted adult in my life. Now a crazy woman was talking about me being the father of her kids and how to kill her husband.

A few days later on Saturday morning, Noah called and asked me if we could pick up a load of mulch for his mom's garden. I agreed and soon was over at his house unloading the fresh mulch from my truck. It was a hot, humid summer day, and I had not talked to Carol Lynn since our conversation about Fred. As Noah and I were working, a familiar-looking black Ford minivan pulled up. Carol Lynn got out, claiming she had been in the area and decided to stop by to see Noah's mom. I had never even seen the two talking before, but there she was, doing just that.

Noah and I finished up and told his mom that we were heading to the self-serve car wash to clean out my truck. Carol Lynn said she suddenly remembered something she had to get done, said her goodbyes, and quickly made her way to her van. As we pulled into the car wash, Carol Lynn was right behind us. I drove into the first available bay, and Noah and I got out of the truck to wash it out. As Noah was putting quarters into the slot to activate the powerwash, Carol Lynn rolled down her window to speak to me. "Get in," she said to me, and I obeyed. Noah looked confused but continued to wash the truck.

Carol Lynn drove around for several minutes as I laid on the bench seat in the back to avoid someone seeing us together. Eventually she turned onto a long driveway surrounded by thick woods on both sides. About a quarter of a mile in, she pulled over, and we got out and went into the woods. I experienced many more firsts that day, including learning what a yeast infection was and what it was like kissing someone after they had performed oral sex on you.

As I drove Noah back to his house in silence, a feeling of guilt and shame came over me like I had never felt before. I wanted to get as far away from myself as possible, but I couldn't. As soon as I dropped Noah off, I drove around until I found a pay phone since I didn't have my cell phone with me. I called Carol Lynn and told her that I wanted things between us to stop. She agreed but threatened that if I ever breathed a word of what had happened between us to anyone, she would ruin my life. "Who would believe a rebellious teen over a respected adult?" she said.

That day I vowed to myself that I would never mention what had happened to anyone.

Chapter 5—Aftermath

I still saw the Mathias at least four times a week at church, and our families still got together. Carol Lynn continued staring at me from across the auditorium with sex-crazed eyes and occasionally would pass me notes during orchestra practice. I avoided contact with her as much as possible, but it was inevitable. My parents even noticed how much I hated being around her and encouraged me to not be bitter, to show her Christlike love. They had no idea what was going on in my head. Nobody did—I couldn't tell anyone.

Noah was the only person who knew what had happened, but by the time I put a stop to everything, Noah and I weren't allowed to be friends anymore. My parents wouldn't let us hang out or even talk to each other at church. Because I had changed so much that summer, my parents blamed my friendship with Noah since we had been around each other so much with the business. How could they know he had nothing to do with my behavior? I wanted so desperately to tell them the truth, but I couldn't.

I entered a phase in my life where I had so many mixed emotions and became confused about so many things. Noah had been my best friend since we were ten, and now I had no one close to talk to. I continued to feel dirty and disgusting about Carol Lynn. This woman told me she loved me and that what we had was true love, but was it? How could it be true love and feel so horrible? It was the lowest time of my life up to that point.

In the fall of 1998, I began my senior year depressed and hating my life. I loathed being homeschooled, and church wasn't any better. I still avoided Carol Lynn, who continued initiating contact. Whereas months earlier I was finding ways to sneak around with Carol Lynn, I was now sneaking around trying to find ways to hang out with Noah. Because my family had no clue what had happened, our families still got together occasionally. Carol Lynn even insisted on baking my graduation cake, which I never ate because only God knew what that woman had done with that cake. By the time spring came around, I wanted out of my life so badly. I remember spending days on our couch in the living room, just staring at the walls. That's when God allowed me to meet the Weidmayer family.

The Weidmayers were farmers who lived up the street from us. They were friendly, and I immediately gravitated to them. In a church filled with so many disingenuous people, they seemed like the real deal. So when the father, Roy, asked me if I would like to come over and help him muck out his sheep pen, I jumped on the opportunity.

I remember mucking out that pen like it was yesterday. It was cold out, and the smell of sheep manure stung my nostrils. The manure-mixed straw that we lifted from the pen was so heavy it felt like I was lifting bricks. The work was backbreaking—especially since I had done almost nothing physical over the winter.

We finished several hours later, and Roy invited me to join his family for dinner. After we ate, we all sat around and talked until I had to leave. It was the best time I'd had in several months. I continued to work for Roy for the rest of that spring and all summer. The Weidmayers became an oasis for me, and I spent as much time with them as possible. Being around my family, my sister's friends, and church members was miserable. I wanted to scream to everyone about my abuse, but I couldn't talk about it.

To make matters worse, Carol Lynn was now stalking me at church and finding ways to communicate with me. I had changed so much in the past year that I was now labeled a rebel among the congregation, which made any friendships impossible. I had had three close friends my age growing up, but one had quit attending our church after Preacher called him out in public for not singing during the song service, another wasn't allowed to talk to me per his parents, and I still wasn't allowed to speak with Noah. I was lonely and misunderstood by those who thought they knew me best. But when I was with the Weidmayers, everything was different. They knew me as the person I was at that time, not a year or five years ago, and they accepted me as that person.

Although I enjoyed being with them and working on the farm, the main reason I kept spending time with them was because of their oldest daughter, Jill. Jill was my age and the opposite of Carol Lynn. Carol Lynn was loud and boisterous. She aggressively pursued me and made me do things I didn't want to do. She was taller than me and big boned. She was jealous and a sociopath. Jill, on the other hand, was quiet and shy. She was beautiful and one of the kindest people I have ever known. As petite as she was, she could outwork most men I know.

That summer, I decided to ask Jill out—a huge deal since I had never done anything like that before. One day after we finished mowing a hayfield and right before I absolutely had to leave, I got Jill alone and asked her if I could take her out on a double date with her brother and his girlfriend. I couldn't believe it when she said yes. I took Jill on several dates during the rest of that summer. I always had to lie to my family because I wasn't allowed to date.

As the summer came to an end, I had to decide where to go to college. I was given two choices—a local Christian college or a newer college in Wisconsin that was owned and operated by Preacher's brother-in-law. I didn't like either choice, but one involved not being around Carol Lynn four times a week. Besides, when my parents suspected that I liked Jill, they lifted the friendship ban with Noah, who wanted to attend the out-of-state college as well. So as much as it pained me to leave behind Jill, working on the farm, and being around people who truly accepted me for who I was, I decided to attend the college in Wisconsin.

Two days before Noah and I left, I spent an entire day with Jill. We shopped, went out to lunch, and took pictures together. Before I left, I held Jill's hand and kissed her. Since then I've liked a lot of girls. I've probably even loved a few. But my first and only true love experience until I met my wife, Emily, was during the summer of '99 when I dated Jill. I will be forever thankful that God allowed me to meet Jill and her family when He did. Things could have turned out very differently if our paths hadn't crossed.

A popular New Testament verse quoted at many weddings is 1 Corinthians 13:4–7: "Love is patient and kind; love does not envy or boast; it is not arrogant or rude. It does not insist on its own way; it is not irritable or resentful; it does not rejoice at wrongdoing, but rejoices with the truth. Love bears all things, believes all things, hopes all things, endures all things." This was the kind of love I experienced with Jill and her family.

As I drove the eighteen miles home that last time seeing Jill, I was devastated that it would be months before I would see her again. I thought that the worst part of college would be the several hundred miles that separated Jill and me. I couldn't have been more wrong.

Chapter 6—College

When Noah and I arrived at school, I was glad to finally get away from all the controlling, judgmental people in my life. It didn't take long to realize that I had made a huge mistake.

The leaders of my Bible college expected the student body to follow every extreme rule and regulation from my church, and then some. We had a stricter dress code—men were not allowed to wear jeans—and stricter rules regarding what we could listen to and watch. We couldn't date, and only juniors or seniors were allowed to court. Even then, the rules were entirely unreasonable, including chaperoned phone calls and in-person time together. All students had to fill out a weekly accountability form saying we had read at least four chapters in the Bible every day, prayed, and went witnessing for two hours every week.

I pity the pastor-president, the staff, and the faculty who ran this college when I attended. I believe most of the people I've known over the years aren't evil but rather people with good hearts that made mistakes. But I truly believe that the president and most of his family, the vice president, and the youth pastor at the church associated with the college at that time were evil people with evil intentions. I hope and pray that they have changed for not only their sake but the sake of the many lives they have destroyed.

My first semester went by quickly. When I wasn't studying, sleeping, or eating, I was handwriting letters to Jill and sneaking away every Saturday night to call her. In the middle of the semester, Noah and I drove home to see our families for the weekend. Before dropping me off at home, Noah took me to see

Jill since our relationship was still secret, and I wouldn't have seen her otherwise.

That Sunday morning at church, Carol Lynn walked right up to me. "How *are* you?" she exclaimed. "How have you been? Your dad has refused to give me your contact information, so I haven't been able to keep in touch to find out how you are or how to pray for you!"

I quickly muttered, "I'm not allowed to talk to you," and darted outside. Earlier that year I had been helping my dad in the back fields, and the guilt of what had happened with Carol Lynn had overwhelmed me to the point I had to tell him. When my dad gave me his word that he wouldn't repeat what I was about to tell him, I blurted out the entire story. So when I was off to college and Carol Lynn "innocently" approached him to ask for my contact information so she could know how to better pray for me, he refused.

Seeing Carol Lynn stirred up emotions I had suppressed for months, and I started to become confused about my direction in life. I had always been brought up believing that ministry was the highest calling. We were groomed by our church leaders to be preachers, evangelists, and missionaries. "If God calls you to the ministry, don't stoop to be the president of the United States," we were told over and over. As a junior in high school, I had planned on following my father's footsteps and joining the Marine Corps as soon as I turned seventeen. I had absolutely no desire to be in the ministry.

But a few months into a college that only offered classes to prepare someone for the ministry, I began to think that even if I wanted to be a pastor or an evangelist, I would be disqualified because of everything that had happened with Carol Lynn. I thought I had blown it and that God could never use me. Suddenly, the desire to be in the ministry, to be all that

God wanted me to be, consumed me. I was tired of sneaking my "worldly" music around and of lying on my weekly accountability form. I was over having to lie to my parents about my relationship with Jill. I just wanted a "clean heart and a new start." This meant I would have to break up with Jill, but if that was what it took for me to be right with God and used by Him, then that's what I was willing to do.

A few days after my epiphany, we left for Christmas break. Once again, Noah took me to see Jill before he dropped me off at home, this time for me to break up with her. It was awkward, but I was excited knowing that now God was going to use me. I would find a godly girl my parents approved of, and we could be in the ministry together. I regret the way I handled my breakup with Jill, who was godlier than any girl I had ever known. I hurt her, and I hurt her family. I felt like a huge weight had been lifted off my shoulders. I went home and "unloaded the truck"—a term our church used when a teen confessed all their sins to their parents or authorities, which included my relationship with Jill—and told my parents that I wanted to be in full-time ministry as a music director. They were ecstatic, and we had the best Christmas ever.

The next semester flew by. Noah had been kicked out the first semester because of finances and perceived nonconformity to the rules, so I was flying solo and loving it. Even though the pickings were slim, I spent my spare time trying to figure out which girl would be the lucky Mrs. Woodbury, wife of music pastor Justin Woodbury. Enough time had passed with Carol Lynn that I was hopeful nobody would ever find out my terrible secret, although it still haunted me daily. Then, right before spring break, my dad called. He explained that Carol Lynn was beginning to target other boys in our church and begged me to tell Preacher what happened. "It wasn't your fault. You won't get in trouble," he told me over and over. Finally, I reluctantly agreed to warn Preacher about Carol Lynn.

A few days after I came home for spring break, I went to breakfast with Preacher and casually brought up the Mathia family.

"By the way, you might want to keep an eye on Mrs. Mathia," I said. "A few years back she acted inappropriately with me, and I think she likes young boys."

"What do you mean she acted inappropriately?" he asked.

"You know, she just wasn't appropriate with me."

"Did she ever touch you?"

"Yes."

"Above the waist or below the waist?"

"Umm, below the waist."

"In the front or in the back?"

"In . . . the front."

"Inside the pants, or outside?"

"I-i-i-inside," I said, trembling, my heart pounding out of my chest.

This kind of questioning went on for twenty more minutes. Toward the end of our conversation, Preacher started asking details I was not willing to give, so I started lying. When the interrogation was finished, Preacher assured me that I had equal blame in this situation because I could have chosen to be like Joseph in Genesis 39, who fled when another woman came on to him. Instead, I had chosen to act like the fool in Proverbs 7.

Then he told me this: "Justin, over the next several weeks and maybe months, I'm going to ask you to do things you might not understand or even agree with. One of the signs of true repentance is one's willingness to do whatever their authority tells them to do. Even if I'm wrong in what I'm telling you to do, as long as you obey me, God will protect you and bless you. Okay?"

I agreed. Then he informed me I couldn't sing in the choir, play in the orchestra, or teach Sunday School until he told me otherwise. He immediately scheduled a meeting with Fred and Carol Lynn and confronted her with my story, which she strongly denied. After more pushing, she broke down and admitted that something did happen, but that I forced myself on her and that she was the victim. Finally, Carol Lynn admitted to everything I told Preacher. By that time, I was already back at college finishing up my freshman year. When I returned home, it seemed like I was in weekly meetings with either Preacher, the deacons, or my parents to sort through what had happened and how it happened, and to make sure I was truly repentant.

Part of my repentance was to meet with Fred and apologize to him for stealing his wife and defiling her. I'll never forget apologizing to Fred. He looked at me in disgust and told me in no uncertain terms how he felt about me and the entire situation. I was ashamed. Carol Lynn also had to meet with my parents and apologize for her part in what took place. And just like that, it was over.

The Mathias wanted to leave the church, but Preacher told them to stay. Eventually they did leave. After a few months, I had regained my positions at church. By law, Preacher was required to report what had happened to the police, but he never did. Carol Lynn should have gone to jail, but she never did. Preacher should have warned the pastor of the next church the Mathias attended, but he never did. But all that pales in comparison to the counseling I should have received, but never did. I don't know why nobody thought a traumatized minor who had been sexually abused by a trusted married woman twice his age would ever need counseling. Maybe the thought never occurred to anyone. Perhaps it was because the extent of counseling in our church was to ensure someone was truly broken and repentant of their sin; in that case, I received plenty of counseling.

Another reason could be that a counselor can lose their license for failing to uphold their duty as a mandatory reporter, and reporting what had happened to the law would have reflected poorly on our church. I believe, though, that the biggest reason I never received any counseling was that the authorities in my life at the time saw me as having equal blame. It didn't matter what the law said. In their minds, I could have been a Joseph, and I wasn't. I could have said no, and I didn't. I stole from another man by taking his wife. I hadn't been reading my Bible or praying during that time. I'd been listening to rock music, which got my mind thinking about sex. I was a rebel. I had quenched the Holy Spirit.

I believed I was to blame, and I hated myself. I had always struggled with insecurity growing up, but after everything with Carol Lynn, my insecurity spiraled out of control. I turned to eating to ease the pain and guilt I felt, and over the next twenty years, I gained over a hundred pounds. I blamed my weight gain on a bad metabolism, on my thyroid, on "just getting old," but the truth was that I didn't respect or even like myself.

Constant reminders of the situation resurfaced my shame and anger. For example, every time I heard the introduction to the hymn "Day by Day," which we sang regularly at church and at college, my heart started pounding, my palms instantly became sweaty, and I became short of breath. Sometimes I would clench my jaw in anger, other times I would just try to fight back tears. When the tears won, I would leave so no one could see me. I hated Carol Lynn with every bit of emotion inside me. I often fantasized about how I would kill her and get away with it. I carried this baggage unknowingly for over twenty years.

A few months after my apology to Carol Lynn's husband, I started my sophomore year. I was thrilled once again to be away from the shame I felt by so many people knowing what I had done, but that was short lived. About a month after college started, Preacher called me up and told me that I had to tell the president what I had done with Carol Lynn. "It's for your protection," he said.

So I did, and the president shared it with the faculty and staff—at least some of them. And just like I was marked as "used goods" at home, I became marked as the same at college. As much as I hated that, I felt like I deserved it, so I went along with it. I never would have made it through those four years if I'd had a shred of self-respect, but I didn't. So I graduated in 2003 with a piece of paper from an unaccredited college that said I had a bachelor's degree in music and moved back home.

A few weeks after I got home, my parents went to Alaska for a month, where my dad would be training for his new job. He had retired as the vice president of operations at the airline and had gone over to the dark side—the FAA. They asked me to come, but I declined. We weren't getting along because they disapproved of the girl I was interested in, but I told them the reason was that I needed to find a job.

The day my parents left, I went to the video store and rented six VHS movies. I was out of college, so I didn't have to abide by their rules (I had almost been expelled for watching an episode of *Get Smart* my senior year), and I wasn't working for a church yet. I had a month to catch up on hundreds of movies I had heard about over the years from "bad" friends at church. So I started watching those movies in the early afternoon, stopping only to order pizza, and finished around four the next morning.

Then I woke up around one o'clock in the afternoon, returned the videos, and rented six more. I started watching those in the early afternoon, again stopping only for pizza. I repeated that cycle nearly every day for the entire month.

When my parents returned from Alaska, I began to get serious about finding a job. I really wanted to be the music pastor at my home church, but because Preacher and some church family friends also strongly disliked the girl I was courting, I doubted that would ever happen. It didn't work out with the girl, though, so I found myself meeting with Preacher to inquire about the position. Our church already had a music director—Jim, one of the most faithful men I've ever known. He had started the choir at our church twenty years earlier and with almost no music training had brought it far. Although music was his passion, he had other responsibilities in the church, so Preacher considered my proposal.

When word got around that I might become the new music pastor, Jim's sister-in-law Sharon, who was a dear friend, took me out to lunch and very strongly advised me not to take that position. She told me that Preacher was a tyrant and control freak, and that I would be miserable. I chalked it up to her just looking out for Jim as well as his sweet wife, Louise, the main piano player and Sharon's sister. Reflecting back, I truly believe Sharon had my best interest at heart.

A few weeks later it became official—I would work part time at a local Christian school and part time at my home church with Preacher and Pastor B, two of my favorite people. I was beyond thrilled. Little did I know that the next six years would be like hell on earth.

Chapter 7—Preacher

There were good times during my role as music pastor. I loved working with the adult, teen, and children's choirs and the orchestra. Going over music and directing cantatas and other special music we performed during the song service is something I'll always cherish. I poured my heart and soul into the music program and made friends that have withstood the test of time. Although I was young and inexperienced, my choir was so gracious with me and allowed me to learn from my mistakes. Jim, the former music director, joined the choir, and even though there were a couple of rough years between us, Jim and Louise became some of my biggest supporters. The choirs and orchestra worked hard, and together we took the music program to a completely different level. We had one of the best in the area, and even though I don't take credit for it, I loved being part of it.

But all the good could never outweigh the bad I suffered behind the scenes—in part because of personal circumstances in Preacher's life. During my years as the music pastor, Preacher's wife, Joy, was in a fight for her life battling cancer. As a fellow husband, I can't imagine what he must have been going through. Joy miraculously escaped death several times but eventually succumbed to the disease. Toward the end of her life, Preacher cared for her in the most loving, gentle way and was heartbroken when she took her last breath. I believe that much, if not all, of the abuse coming from Preacher during this time stemmed from his own hurt. I also wouldn't be surprised if he was going through a mental breakdown. So today, my heart is free from bitterness, anger, or resentment.

Before it became official that I would be the new music pastor, Preacher met with my parents. He told them that if they ever interfered with how he dealt with me as my pastor and my boss, I would immediately be fired. They were not allowed to go to Preacher about anything they disagreed with regarding me.

Preacher also met with me to tell me that my parents did not do a great job raising me and that he was having to pick up where they left off, and "oh, boy," did he have his work cut out for him. Preacher told me I was lazy and had a horrible work ethic. He convinced me that if it weren't for the fact that he was gracious enough to give me a job, I would be out on the streets. He criticized everything I did and never complimented me. He would say, "If you're looking for someone to pamper you and tell you that you've done a good job, find another boss."

More often than not, he was angry and downright mean. He demanded loyalty and obedience and would lose his mind if he didn't get both. He was excellent at using the Bible to back up any point he was trying to make, and if you had a different point, he would often slam his fist down on his desk and say, "Why are you arguing with me?" He had a group of yes men as his deacons, so when push came to shove, not one of them dared to go against him.

Preacher was the most controlling person I've ever known. He controlled when I went to the bathroom on church nights, how I sat during his sermons, and whether I could have my sleeves rolled up while he was preaching. Twice he criticized and made fun of me from the pulpit—once on my weight, another time on how I prayed. I already knew he was very critical of dress, especially women's. Each week he would meet with me and tell me that someone's dress was either too short, too low cut, too tight, or too see through. He was so obsessed that he literally looked each woman he came across up and down to judge her clothes.

Preacher also believed that if you weren't participating in the song service, you were a rebel. We used to spend hours talking about the way different people in the congregation sang. One time he mentioned a teen who barely moved her lips: "She's a rebel. Mark my words, that girl is trouble." Years later I would find out that the entire time that "rebel" was attending our church, she was being molested by her father. During the same conversation, Preacher pointed out a man and a woman and said they must be filled with the Holy Spirit because they sang as if they were in the very presence of God Himself. Months later, that man was fired from his job at the sheriff's office for looking at porn on his work computer. The woman he mentioned was in the middle of a twelve-year affair with a married man in our church.

I started noticing Preacher's bend toward abuse and control not long after I began working at the church. One incident involved my dad borrowing wood off the church land for my parents' woodburning stove, which heated part of their house during the winter. Our church sat on forty acres, a large part of that being woods. Preacher had decided to thin out the woods, so one day he and I marked the trees he wanted cut down with paint, and he gave my dad permission to cut them down for firewood. Preacher also had a fireplace and would come over sometimes in the winter and load up from my dad's supply.

One Saturday my dad and I loaded up our truck and trailer and drove to the church to cut down some of the marked trees. For some reason, I thought that a big, beautiful oak right on the edge of the woods was one of the trees Preacher wanted to get rid of. So my dad started up the chainsaw and began cutting down that oak tree. Suddenly Preacher was there screaming, and I mean screaming, at me.

"What do you think you are doing? Who told you to cut this tree down? Don't you realize this is an oak tree? Are you stupid?"

I profusely apologized over and over, but the more I apologized, the angrier Preacher became. He was like a madman, out of control. My dad, trying to calm Preacher down, said, "Hey, Preacher, it's only a tree," but Preacher turned his anger toward my dad and told him to get off the church property. "I'm not going anywhere, and if you don't like that, you can leave," Dad responded. Then Preacher got in his car and drove off. About an hour later he showed back up in the church truck, rolled down his window, and demanded that I get in. For the next twenty minutes, we drove around the country roads while he laid me out some more.

Because the church couldn't afford to bring me on full time as the music pastor, I worked Monday through Thursday doing maintenance and spent Friday working in the office on music. Every Tuesday Preacher took a break from studying and preparing sermons and helped Pastor B and me with maintenance or building projects. He worked hard and expected everyone else to work at his same pace. The year before, however, I had major surgery to correct a herniated disc in my lower back. The recovery was six months, and I was told I could never lift anything over fifty pounds again. So I did my best given the circumstances, but my best was never good enough. I never worked fast enough, hard enough, smart enough for Preacher. He constantly berated my work ethic. It didn't matter to him that I wasn't supposed to do any heavy lifting.

Several times I had relapses with my back because of working by Preacher's side. One particular time he was having me dig around a tree so we could spread mulch. Because the ground was clay, we had to break it up with a pickax before we could dig it out. As I was swinging the pickax, I threw my back and immediately fell to my knees in excruciating pain. I told Preacher I needed to leave, but he wouldn't let me. "You don't have to use the pickax, but I want you to shovel the dirt in the wheelbarrow," he said.

When Preacher realized I couldn't do that, he made me wheelbarrow the clay to the edge of the woods and dump it. After a few trips, I begged Preacher to let me go home, but he still wouldn't let me. Instead, he made me stand there and watch him continue to work. That was the first time I can remember wondering that Preacher might be right about my work ethic. I felt small standing there while he was working so hard.

It seemed like Preacher was always trying to break me, to undue all twenty-plus years of my parents raising me and start from scratch. He reminded me on a regular basis of my parents' failure to raise me right, using my "unruly" behavior as an excuse to control so much of my life, especially at church. During one of our weekly meetings where we would go over how the previous Sunday went and plan for the next Sunday, he asked me why I didn't go straight to my seat when I walked down from the pulpit. I explained that after leading congregational singing, directing the choir and orchestra, and sometimes singing special music, I would be hot and sweaty, so I always went to the restroom and washed my face and hands before returning back to my seat.

"No more," Preacher said. "You're not setting a good example for everyone else. From now on, you have to go right from the pulpit to your seat. Also, you aren't allowed to roll up your sleeves during church anymore or sit with your arms on the back of the seat. It makes you look like you think you are a cool dude."

Another time Preacher told me that his wife had counted thirteen times that I had looked away from him and toward a certain family, and he wanted to know why. During these meetings I was also confronted about my Facebook account, my friends, my family, how much time I spent on the phone, the way I dressed, my hair, and my leather jacket. (Every time I wore my leather jacket, Preacher rattled off a list of two or three pastors he knew who wore leather jackets and had to step down from the ministry because of impropriety.)

Preacher also tried to control who I married. A family who attended our church had a very sweet daughter my age. She was probably the most talented piano player in our church, and Preacher believed I should marry her. There was only one small problem—I was not attracted to this young lady at all. I explained this to Preacher in several of our meetings, but he would always shake his head and respond, "Justin, I believe Sarah is the Lord's will for you. It doesn't matter if you're attracted to her. If she's the right one, you'll learn to become attracted to her."

I did my best to submit to Preacher's abusive control of me, but from time to time I would get discouraged and depressed. One of my "life verses" during that time was 1 Peter 2:18: "Servants, be subject to your masters with all respect, not only to the good and gentle but also to the unjust." A well-meaning elder in the church had pointed that verse out to me one time when he observed Preacher's abuse and told me I had to submit myself to Preacher because that's what the Bible says, and the Lord would bless me for doing so.

One weekend when I was discouraged and reflecting on that verse and other verses about submitting myself to my elders, I made up my mind that even though I couldn't control the way

Preacher acted toward me, I could control my response. It was an epiphany, and I was excited to put that lesson to practical use.

I remember that Sunday morning anxiously waiting for Preacher to join me on the platform before church started. As soon as he sat down, I took a big breath and blurted out, "I need to ask your forgiveness for something. You see, I've been having a bad attitude recently because I have been rebelling against some of the rules you've given me. But God showed me over the weekend that you're not the problem, that I'm the problem. This weekend I learned that I can't control what you tell me to do or how you treat me, but I can control my response. And recently my attitude has been horrible, and I would like to ask your forgiveness. From now on, no matter what you tell me or how you treat me, I am going to have a good attitude."

I waited for Preacher's response. He had been staring straight ahead the entire time, and I wasn't sure he had even heard me. But then I saw a smirk develop on his stern face and he said, "So you mean to tell me that no matter how I treat you that you will have a good attitude?"

"Absolutely!" I responded with a smile.

"Yeah . . . okay, we'll see about that," Preacher sneered.

That next Tuesday was particularly hot and humid. Media outlets all over warned anyone working outside to take it easy. The dew point was so high that just standing outside caused sweating in places I didn't even know sweat pours existed. I'll never forget that day. Preacher decided that we should landscape the church grounds, which was important to him because he kept his own lawn and garden pristine and always wanted our church to have great curbside appeal. That day he pushed me both physically and mentally harder than he ever had and made fun of my weight and work ethic. This was Preacher's way of trying to break me. Although I had promised myself that I would have a good attitude no matter what, by the end of the day, I was done. Preacher knew it too; he walked past me and said, "So much for your good attitude no matter what."

One of the many areas where Preacher believed my parents fell short in raising me was their lack in telling me no, and he was determined to fix it. As a result, when I would ask for something I needed permission for, such as time off, leaving early, or borrowing a church tool, Preacher would randomly say no. One particular time was around Father's Day. My parents decided to fly to Boston to visit my grandpa, whose health was failing, and they invited me along. The plan was to celebrate Father's Day with Grandpa as well as my mom's birthday, which happened to be around the same time. It was probably going to be my grandpa's last Father's Day, and I was excited to be able to spend some time with him.

When I went to Preacher to request that time off, he simply said, "No." When I asked why not, he responded with the familiar "your parents told you yes too many times" speech. Not knowing what to do, I walked out of his office and called my parents to tell them I couldn't go. My parents were crushed, but they had agreed to stay out of Preacher's and my business, so they canceled my ticket. Normally that would have been the end of it, but I couldn't stop thinking about how important it was to my parents and grandpa for me to be with them during that time. So I very humbly and cautiously went back to Preacher a few days later to ask him to reconsider. I told him I believed it was the Lord's will for me to go and asked him if he would pray about it.

"Why do you think it's the Lord's will for you to go?" he asked.

"Because my parents want me to go, and I believe that the Lord would have me honor them in this way," I responded.

Preacher shook his head just like he had done hundreds of times before and said, "Oh, Justin, you're overlooking one important detail. I already told you no. Tell me, how is it possible for your trip to be the Lord's will when your pastor told you no? The Lord doesn't contradict himself. In other words, it's not possible for me to be against this trip *and* for it to be the Lord's will. My answer is firm—*no*."

When I saw my parents next, I shared my conversation with them. The only time my parents ever went to Preacher on my behalf was for this situation. At the risk of me losing my job because of their agreement, they pleaded with Preacher to let me spend time with them and my ill grandfather. The answer was still no. Out of desperation I even went to the head deacon, who immediately met with Preacher and strongly recommended that he let me go.

The next time Preacher saw me, he called me into his office. "I still believe it's not the Lord's will for you to go to Boston with your parents," he said. "However, you, your parents, and now the head deacon are all against me on this, so this is what I'm going to do. I'm going to leave the decision up to you. But know this—if you decide to go against what I've told you, you probably won't have a job when you return. I can't have someone on my staff who doesn't follow the leading of the Holy Spirit through their God-ordained authorities. So go ahead and go. Good luck finding another job."

That was all I needed to make a final decision. I called my parents and told them I couldn't go. A few months later, my grandpa died.

In the six years I worked under Preacher, I stood up to him only twice. One time was when he called me out publicly for talking during a prayer meeting. I can't remember the circumstances surrounding the second time, but I do remember meeting with him in his office and telling him that I couldn't continue to work for someone like him. He told me to quit if I didn't like the way he treated me. At that point, quitting sounded like the best option, so I told him that I would like to resign. He laughed at me and said, "You will never find another job. You are lazy and irresponsible. You are lucky I haven't fired you yet. You'll find out very quickly how good you had it here. But go ahead—quit. I'll meet with the deacons to make it official."

Before I left, he asked me to explain what I meant when I said I couldn't work for someone like him. I told him he didn't exhibit many of the fruits of the Spirit—love, joy, peace, patience, kindness, goodness, faithfulness, gentleness, and self-control (Galatians 5:22). I left Preacher's office feeling relieved on one hand but scared to death on the other hand. I kept wondering if I had signed my own death warrant employment wise. I was raking in $24,000 per year. Would I ever be able to find another job making that much?

The next night at church when Preacher got up to preach, he started off with, "Please turn your Bibles to Galatians 5:22. Recently, I was accused of not exhibiting the fruit of the Spirit, so tonight I want to go over each fruit and explain what exhibiting that fruit really looks like." For the next hour, Preacher explained that passage so different from how I had ever heard it explained before that by the end, nobody would have questioned whether he was filled with the Spirit. In fact, I was so convicted about accusing this godly man of not being Spirit filled that I could barely make it through directing the invitational song without breaking down crying.

After the invitation, I immediately asked to meet with Preacher in his office. As soon as his door closed, I burst into tears and begged him to forgive me. "I'm the problem, not you," I sobbed. "You have been so gracious and kind to me. I don't deserve to work under you, and if you would see fit, it would be a privilege to call you my boss. You're right. I am lazy and irresponsible. I'm a bad employee and should have been fired a long time ago. I'm so sorry. Please forgive me. I promise I'll do better."

So Preacher allowed me to continue to work at the church, but he put me on probation for six months, which meant I feared that every day there would be my last. Also, I had to write down everything I did in fifteen-minute increments and turn my report in every week.

After that, I never even entertained the thought of quitting my job. I was convinced that Preacher was my lifeline—that if it weren't for him putting up with how terrible of an employee I was, I would be living on the streets. Preacher had me right where he wanted me—he knew I was terrified to lose my job and used it to constantly torture me and play mind games with me.

One opportunity he took advantage of involved a girl I liked. Every morning before we started working, Preacher, Pastor B, and I met to pray for about a half hour. One morning when Pastor B was out of town, Preacher confronted me. "I went over to John and Cindy's house last night, and if what he told me about you is true, then you'll be fired with no questions asked."

"What did he say?" I asked, confused.

"Something not good at all!" he replied.

"What? Please tell me." My heart was pounding, and I was racking my brain trying to think what John could possibly be talking about.

"You'll find out when we meet John for lunch today at twelve. In the meantime, you are *not* allowed to contact him to find out what we talked about. You better just hope and pray that it was all a big misunderstanding."

Those next four hours were the longest of my entire life. My heart never returned to resting rate, and my entire body was shaking all morning. I couldn't get any work done; I kept replaying every scenario in my mind involving John and how it could have been misunderstood. It was torture. I swore I aged ten years that morning.

As it turned out, it was all a big misunderstanding—John had overheard me on the phone telling someone I loved them and assumed it was Megan, a girl in the church I had liked for several years. It was actually my mom. Because it was considered mentally and emotionally impure to express feelings of love toward a girl I wasn't courting, Preacher was going to fire me.

Although it seemed like Preacher especially enjoyed abusing me, he was an equal opportunity abuser. Every member of our church was subject to not only Preacher's authoritarian abuse but also his psychological abuse. As a result, his abusive behavior became a pattern for parents' behavior toward their children. One of the most devastating examples of this played out with a young man named Joey.

Chapter 8—Joey

Joey grew up in our church. He was quiet and one of the most respectful kids in our youth group. Even though he kept to himself, Joey was kind to others, and I never saw him in an argument with his peers. Regardless, he was considered a "passive rebel" by the church leaders, meaning his rebellion was secret and therefore harder to detect.

I got to know Joey when he joined the teen choir and then began to excel on the piano. He was naturally gifted and worked diligently to learn his music. As he progressed, I used him more for playing the piano in my choirs and was excited to see how God would use him in the future.

Once in a while in the summer, some of the teen choir members would come out to the church during the week to help us with our bigger outdoor projects—spreading wood chips around hundreds of pine trees the church staff had planted years earlier, mowing several acres of grass, and watering plants. We would treat the teens to lunch and give them twenty dollars each—it was a win-win. Sometimes Joey would come out and help. Having grown up without a father, Joey lacked the knowledge to do even some of the most essential tasks for a boy his age, so I tried to take him under my wing and show him how to do things like check the oil in the church truck and change out a flat tire. As he got older, I even let him drive the church truck all over the property to practice learning to drive. I always enjoyed my time with the teens, and Joey was no exception.

One Wednesday night after church, a few of the youth group girls approached me in tears, pleading for my help. They had caught Joey swallowing a handful of ibuprofen from the first aid kit we had stored in our fellowship hall. When I found Joey, he was sitting on a table surrounded by several of his friends. He seemed both nervous and calm. I took Joey aside and asked him why he had just swallowed the pills. What Joey told me next still haunts me to this day: because he had disrespected his mom at church, he was told he would be spanked when he got home. Joey was seventeen.

Corporal punishment was practiced and encouraged in our church. "Spare the rod, spoil the child," we were taught. A popular verse we referred to regarding corporal punishment was Proverbs 23:13: "Withhold not correction from the child: for if thou beatest him with the rod, he shall not die" (KJV). Despite having no children, Preacher spoke regularly on child rearing and counseled many parents regarding their rebellious teen children. Because of this mentality, I was spanked until I was sixteen, and my parents only stopped because I convinced them that they could no longer hurt me. I'll never forget my last spanking. I had back-talked my mom, and she sent me to the bathroom while she grabbed the wooden dowel rod. I was told to bend over and grab the bathroom vanity, and I did so with a smile. Although the pain was excruciating, I forced that smile throughout the entire session. When my mom was finished, I smirked at her and said, "Thank you. I needed that more than you know." Then I walked out of the bathroom whistling. When my mom realized her best attempts were ineffective, she began grounding me as punishment instead.

Compared to some of my friends, I was young when I received my last spanking. I knew kids who were eighteen, nineteen, and sometimes twenty years old when they received theirs. I even knew one girl who was spanked on the night before her wedding because she disrespected her father. When my wife, Emily, was in her midtwenties, her father, who had a history of serious physical abuse, threatened to spank her during a disagreement.

Most parents would spank their kids with a wooden spatula or a foot-long glue stick as many as fifty times for the more "sinful" actions. This was not what Joey described would happen to him, though. At six feet tall, Joey would be instructed to pull his pants down, bend over, and grab his ankles, at which point his mom would begin spanking him. Sometimes the spanking lasted only four to five minutes. Other times, it would last ten or even fifteen minutes. He said the first several minutes were the worst, but after that, he just got numb. The pills were for the pain he would experience several hours later when feeling started to kick back in. He would have to rub petroleum jelly on his backside because of the bleeding and cracking.

As I took all of this in, a knot formed in my stomach. I made up my mind that even if half of it were true, something needed to be done. The first opportunity I had the next day, I called our head deacon and invited him to lunch. He too was horrified and agreed that we needed to take action. We decided that the next step was for me to talk to Preacher about this.

It was still another day before I was able to sit down with Preacher to describe in detail what I had found out about Joey's abuse earlier that week. I poured my heart out to Preacher on Joey's behalf that day. When I finished, Preacher laughed. I'll never forget what he told me next: "Justin, obviously Joey's mom isn't spanking hard enough or long enough because Joey is a rebel. He doesn't have the joy of the Lord on his face, and he hardly sings during the song service." And that was the end of the conversation. Preacher had made his decision, and nothing more was ever brought up. Looking back, I wish I had done more to intercede for Joey. Nobody was stopping me from reporting that kind of inexcusable abuse to the police. Sadly, that thought never even crossed my mind. For almost thirty years, I had been taught to obey those in authority, even if they were wrong.

I wish I could say that this was the only time I was privy to physical abuse, but it wasn't. When I was a junior in college, I interned as a music director at the church that ran the college. There were two other interns: the pastor's son and a guy who attended a different college. At least one night a week, members of the church would have the three of us over for a meal so they could get to know us. During one such dinner at a young family's house, the toddler was a bit fussy. Later that evening as we were driving home, the pastor's son, Stephen, remarked at how thankful he was that his parents didn't let him get away with stuff like that. He then hung his head and said, "I'm ashamed to tell you this, but there was this one time . . ."

Stephen proceeded to tell us a story about when he was younger. He and his older, mentally disabled brother had been entertaining themselves by going through the phone book and calling random numbers, then hanging up. At one point their mom had walked in on them and was so upset she told them that they would be getting one thousand spankings each. I interrupted Stephen to make sure I didn't misunderstand the number; he was quick to reassure me that yes, this was the correct number—after all, they had no business prank calling people like that! Then he sort of chuckled and told us how she had to take a break after every two hundred spankings, and after six hundred, she became exhausted and quit.

Later that fall, Joey was going to be attending the same college I had attended. I hoped that a brighter future was in store for him despite the way he was raised and where he was headed, and that by God's will, he would go on to do great things. He never got that chance. A few months later, he was involved in a drowning accident and died. The day after Joey's accident, as we were reflecting on such a horrible tragedy in our weekly staff meeting, Preacher concluded that God had "taken Joey home" as a wake-up call to all the other rebellious teens in our church.

Joey's situation was clearly child abuse. What's worse, our church not only covered it up but also encouraged it.

One of the results of growing up in a cultlike church that enforced unsustainable rules and encouraged physical beatings as the consequence of breaking those rules was a twisted sense of right and wrong. Since so many "normal" things—like "worldly" music and movies and "immodest" dress such as pants on women—were prohibited but still done in secret, consciences were seared, and lines separating right from wrong became blurred. Because everything was forbidden, the truly forbidden became normalized. And because of the severe, humiliating consequences for sin in our church, we all became master liars and deceivers. This played out with disastrous effects.

One of the clearest examples of deception and the forbidden becoming normal happened over a twelve-year period with two church members—William, a married man, and his administrative assistant, Susan.

Chapter 9—William and Susan

I grew up with Susan. We were less than a year apart, and her family lived only two miles down the road. Our families were very close, and we spent a lot of time at each other's houses. Susan's immediate family and her cousins would swim in our pool in the hot months, and we would always get invited to the cottage that their families would rent for a few weeks every summer. Since we were both homeschooled and lived so close to each other, our families often did extracurricular activities together. I loved Susan, her mom and dad—who was my first Sunday School teacher and whose lessons and illustrations I still remember—and her brothers and sisters, and some of my best memories included her family.

Susan and I remained close friends throughout high school and kept in contact while I was in college. When I graduated and came back to work at church, Susan was in my choir. By this time, our church was already several years into its controlling and sadistic thinking, including its abusive-leaning view on corporal punishment. Perhaps no family took this view to the extreme more than Susan's.

Unbeknownst to many for most of her upbringing, Susan's dad, Jake, had been mentally and emotionally abusing his family for several years. Eventually, the abuse became worse and turned physical. Preacher had been told about it several times. His response was always the same—"Children, obey your parents: honor your father and mother, and God will protect you."

One day the summer I graduated from college, our home phone rang. When I answered it, I thought someone might have had the wrong number because the other end was silent.

Then I heard a terrified whisper begging me for help. I quickly recognized the voice—it was Susan's younger sister. But before I could ask her what was wrong, she had hung up the phone. Without thinking, I grabbed my dad's .38 revolver, jumped into the car, and raced down the road toward their house. Only a few weeks earlier, I had witnessed Susan's dad lose his temper and almost run over two women with his SUV. I was scared for my life.

As I approached the house, I pulled into the driveway next door. A long row of thick, tall, brush separated the two driveways, and I decided to crawl through it to see what was going on. Pretty soon I saw Susan's dad storm out of the house and head toward the pole barn. As he disappeared behind the doors, my mind replayed a conversation I had with Susan earlier that summer. Her dad had lost his temper and began dragging her mom around the house by her hair. At one point he grabbed a gun and headed to the pole barn. Out of fear for her family's life, she had called Preacher, begging him to help. As he had responded many times before, Preacher told Susan she needed to respect, honor, and obey her dad.

Now, kneeling in the bushes with a loaded pistol in my hand, I wondered if Jake had his own gun he planned on using that day. I also wondered if I had been too late—if Jake had already murdered his family. I stayed in those bushes for what seemed like hours, contemplating what to do, but Jake never came out of the pole barn. Eventually I left. The next day I told Preacher what had happened. His only response was to rebuke me for having a gun.

During this time Susan was working for a financial advisor— William, whose family had recently joined our church. William was friendly and personable and had a beautiful family. His wife, Kelly, was one of the sweetest women I knew, and their four children were cute and well behaved. William's family began attending our church about a year before I graduated from college, and they were already an integral part of our church family when I became the music director. William worked in the sound booth, Kelly helped in the nursery, and the kids sang in the children's choir. William's financial business, which he ran out of his home, had grown to the point that he needed administrative help to help offload some of his responsibilities. Susan had recently graduated from college and was looking for work, so when William offered her a job, she took it.

I began getting to know William about a year after I started working at the church. In addition to William's job as a financial advisor, he was also a real estate agent and was always willing to help people out, even if he didn't financially benefit. Because I was looking to move from my parents' house, I asked William to be my buying agent, and he agreed. By that time rumors—also known as prayer requests—began circulating throughout our church about how much time William and Susan were spending together. They seemed to consistently arrive at church at the same time, always parking next to each other. Sometimes Kelly would leave town with the kids for several days, meaning Susan was alone with William at his home office. Susan admitted to her sisters that she frequently took naps in William's bed when she became tired throughout the day.

People also began noticing how much William seemed to obsess about Susan's whereabouts, how his eyes softened whenever he saw her. Susan's boyfriend at the time was so convinced that something extramarital was going on that he pulled William aside and confronted him. William angrily and adamantly denied any impropriety. Me, I was clueless. In fact, I was one of William's biggest defenders. Finding a house I could afford took months, and during that time, I became very close to William and his family. He was sweet to his wife and gentle with his kids. Yes, Susan was over all the time, but I only saw a caring family reaching out to a girl who wanted so badly to be away from her abusive environment. William and his family had almost become Susan's adopted family, I thought. Besides, William had confided in me that he suffered from erectile dysfunction, and wasn't even able to have sex with Kelly.

I began spending at least one evening each week at their house. They fed me dinner, and after the kids went to bed, we watched movies. Usually Susan joined us. When William bought an old farm twenty miles out in the country, I spent several Saturdays helping him move, offloading the majority of their boxes, including most of their family photos, into the barn until the run-down farmhouse was move-in ready.

Shortly after William bought the farmhouse, Susan stopped working for him and got a job downtown. One day a few weeks later, I got a call from Susan's mom.

"Have you heard from Susan today?" she asked me, the panic evident in her voice. "She didn't show up for work, and her phone's going to voicemail."

"No," I told her, concerned about my friend's whereabouts. "I haven't. But I'll let you know if I do."

I kept in touch with Susan's family, cousins, and friends for the rest of the day as they all exhausted their resources trying to find out what happened to her.

Late that night, Susan called me. She told me she had decided to leave town because of her abusive environment. Things had apparently gotten so bad at home that she feared for her life. She wouldn't tell me or anyone else where she was staying or how long she would be gone, just that she was okay.

Susan didn't visit home for several weeks. When she finally did, she was clearly a few months pregnant. Oh, the rumors that spread—mostly about William being the father. I just laughed at them. After all, the man had ED. Of course I was just as curious to know who the father was, but Preacher and the deacons were the only ones who wielded the power to demand the truth. And so the process of Susan's grieving, repentance, and restoration began.

The church secretary, who also happened to be Susan's cousin, was intimately involved in the restoration process and enjoyed exchanging confidential information for favors, which resulted in weekly inside information as to how the process was going. Among the questions surrounding Susan's baby daddy were how many times she had had sex with this man, whether she enjoyed the sex, and how long this had been going on. Susan willingly answered all these questions except for one—who the father was. She made it clear that this was a one-night stand and that she had no desire for this man to be part of her or her baby's life.

However, Preacher and the deacons demanded that she not only reveal who the father was but also tell him that he had a child. If she didn't, she would not be restored in the eyes of the church or to God. For starters, though, they just wanted a name. So Susan gave them a name—Jack. Apparently Jack was a nurse who worked at a local hospital. Susan must not have planned for one of the deacons, also employed by that same hospital, to access its database to confirm that a Jack was even employed there—there wasn't. Susan tried again with another name and another story but got caught lying again. Finally, she gave Preacher and the deacons a name and phone number, which one of the deacons called. When the voicemail matched the same name Susan had provided, he was satisfied and Susan was allowed to repent publicly before the church.

Not long into Susan's pregnancy, William's barn in the country, and everything in it, burned to the ground. The detective on the case ruled the fire as arson, and William was paid one hundred thousand dollars by the insurance company. Once again, rumors circulated about the fire in relationship to Susan, who was not working full time but lived in an apartment and drove a brand-new car.

About eight and a half months into Susan's pregnancy, William invited me over for dinner. When I pulled into their horseshoe driveway, Susan's car was parked in front of the door, so I pulled in behind her. After dinner when the kids were in bed, we all sat down in the living room to watch a movie. Halfway through the movie, Susan suddenly got up and left the house. We all assumed she was tired and had gone home, but a half hour later, she showed back up. When she walked through the front door, William immediately got up from the couch and met her in the hallway.

Kelly paused the movie and we both sat there several minutes while William and Susan spoke in hushed tones by the front door. As I tried to figure out what could be so important that it had to be whispered about, I began to get very uncomfortable. Judging from her expression, Kelly felt the same. For the first time since I had found out Susan was pregnant, I wondered if William might have been involved.

When we finished watching the movie, I went to start Susan's car for her since it was wintertime. When I came back inside, William, Susan, and Kelly were all standing in the front doorway talking. Suddenly, I heard the sound of what I can only describe as a water balloon hitting the ground—Susan's water had broken. Susan burst into tears as Kelly dialed the hospital where Susan was to have her delivery. The doctor told her that unless Susan was having contractions, there wasn't much the hospital could do, at least that night. Based on the doctor's orders, William, Susan, and Kelly decided that Susan would spend the night at their house and make more decisions in the morning.

This is when things started getting bizarre.

William turned to me and said, "Justin, why don't you and Kelly go to Susan's apartment and grab some overnight clothes for her, and I'll stay back here with Susan?" I stood there in the doorway not knowing what to say. *Of all the combinations of who should go and who should stay, why would William pick this one?* I thought to myself. William immediately sensed my hesitation and responded, "Actually, Justin, you just stay here, and Kelly and I will go to Susan's." As soon as they left, Susan began calling her family from the home phone to update them, and I went outside to turn off Susan's car.

As I stepped inside her car, the dome light came on and shined right on Susan's flip phone. On a whim, I picked it up and looked at the text messages. I'll never be able to unsee what I saw. The very first set of texts were so sensual, I blushed just reading them. "Good morning, beautiful, I dreamed about you all night." "Hi, my love, I can't stop thinking about you and longing to hold you in my arms." "I can't wait until one day we can be together." Text after text after text—all between William and Susan.

My heart began to pound out of my chest, and I started getting tunnel vision. My fingers were all thumbs as I tried to turn off Susan's car and make my way back inside the house, where Susan was cheerfully updating her sisters and cousins. I sat on the couch and stared at a wall until William and Kelly showed up several minutes later. Then I quickly excused myself and went home.

Back in college, I was known for my ability to sleep anywhere at any time—in a closet, at my desk, on the floor, on the lawnmower (while it was in park). On the night I read those text messages, for the first time in my life I couldn't go to sleep. I lay in bed for hours trying to make sense of what had just happened. It was clear beyond a shadow of a doubt that William was the father, but now what? Growing up, we had been given very harsh warnings that if we knew about a "sin" and didn't expose it, then we were just as guilty as the one who committed that sin. I didn't want to be guilty of adultery, lying, or fornicating. I was the music director of a well-established church, and I could lose my job if I didn't tell someone. I wished so badly that I hadn't picked up that phone and read those texts. Now I felt that I was responsible for doing something about it—but what?

The next day I poured my heart out to Noah, which gave me some relief to finally be able to tell someone. After that, I decided to take a step back and wait. Abby, Susan's older sister, was getting married in a few months, and there was much to be done to prepare—arranging music, cleaning the church, and planting flowers, just to name a few. It just didn't seem like the right time to bring this up to anyone else.

People came from all over the country to attend Abby's wedding, including some of my friends from college. A few of them stayed with me, and we enjoyed reminiscing about the good old days, even though we had been out of school for only a few years. Johnathan, one of my closest friends in college, and I stayed up late one night, talking in my room. Susan was still a hot topic among our small circle of churches, so eventually the conversation turned to her.

"I know who the father is," I calmly told Johnathan.

"No, you don't!" he replied.

I also had a reputation in college for chasing whims. During the winter of my junior year, Johnathan and I staked out the church we attended to try to find out who had been egging it. After several nights, I saw a group of teens drive behind the building, get out, and start throwing dozens of eggs. I chased them on foot until they got back in their car and drove off. Johnathan and I jumped in my car and took off after them but never found them. That was one of many adventures Johnathan had joined me on, so he was familiar with my whims and knew that oftentimes, they were dead wrong. So I understood his reaction when he didn't believe I knew who the father was.

"Check this out," I said as I reached under my mattress and pulled out a yellow file folder. Enclosed were a handwritten copy of those text messages and a DNA kit I had considered using to confirm William's paternity. My dad was the unofficial church barber, so I could easily get a DNA sample from William's hair. Susan's sisters and cousins, who had long suspected that William and Susan were having an affair, were ready at any time to provide a hair DNA sample from Susan's baby.

As Johnathan read those messages, his jaw dropped. "Who else knows about these text messages?" he demanded.

"Just Noah," I replied.

For the next few hours, Johnathan and I went back and forth about who to tell and when. Johnathan too had been raised to never cover for someone's sin, and now that he was aware of what I knew, he felt a responsibility to expose William and Susan.

"If you don't tell your pastor, I will," he warned.

"Okay," I agreed. "Right after the wedding, I'll tell Preacher." I decided first, though, to talk to Jason, the deacon who worked at the same hospital Susan had claimed the father worked at. When he was finally satisfied that Susan was telling the truth about the father, he was one of her biggest supporters. Jason was opinionated but for the most part balanced, and I wanted to tell him about those text messages first.

As I shared the details with Jason and his wife, Cindy, they listened intently. When I was finished, Jason said, "Justin, I'm not sure what those text messages were about and who they were from, but it's impossible for William to be the father of Susan's baby. As a medical nurse, I was approached by William several months ago about his erectile dysfunction issues he's been experiencing for at least a year. So you see, William can't even have sex, much less get a girl pregnant. Besides, Susan has already satisfied our requirements for knowing who the father is."

Although Jason was being gracious, I was clearly interfering where I didn't belong. Still, I had to tell Preacher as I had agreed. I scheduled a time to meet with him and asked him to keep our conversation confidential. The day we met I told him everything—how we were watching movies, how Susan left and came back and was whispering with William in the hall. I described in detail how William reacted when Susan's water broke, and how I found the text messages on her phone.

When I was done, I took a big breath and waited. I was afraid I would get fired for going into so much detail. I had broken at least two major rules—watching "bad" movies and being alone in the house with another woman. Instead, Preacher responded like Jason. He was satisfied with their investigation and wasn't happy that I was interfering. Basically, I was told to drop it. I left that meeting with more questions than answers. Why was Preacher so ready to dismiss those text messages? Why wouldn't he confront William with that information? Why was he just sweeping this under the rug? Instead of listening to Preacher, I decided to dig into this situation further. *I have an obligation to expose sin!* I convinced myself.

For the next several months, I threw every spare minute into my own investigation. Police and detective work had always fascinated me, and I came at William and Susan as if my life depended on it. I followed them and conducted late-night stakeouts. It was during this time that Susan obtained her real estate license and began selling houses with William. I had a theory that they met up at empty houses they were selling to have sex. One of those houses, William's mother's house, had been empty for months as they were waiting for it to be sold.

One day William called me and asked if I would be willing to pick something up from there with my truck. When I walked inside the house, the first thing I noticed were the oddly satisfying vacuum cleaner lines in the carpet all over the house. I also noticed an area on the dining room carpet that, although clean, had no lines like the rest of the house did. It was about a six-by-six-foot area—*just enough for two people to commit fornication,* I thought to myself. Even though the entire house was immaculate, a box of tissues sat on the floor next to that worn area. When I looked in the kitchen trash, I found several used tissues inside. As I was leaving, I struck up a conversation with the next-door neighbor, who was watering her garden.

"So, do you see William over here a lot?" I asked her casually.

"Oh, all the time," she responded. "Usually he's with his real estate partner."

"You mean his wife?" I inquired.

"No, not Kelly; Susan, his real estate partner."

Susan's sisters and cousins helped with my investigation as well, creating opportunities for me to stick my nose where it didn't belong. During one of those times, I found even more sexually explicit text messages on Susan's phone from William. I never should have looked at Susan's phone the first time, though. It was none of my business, but I thought this was my responsibility and that I was helping God out.

About six months after I told Preacher about the text messages, I was working at church, changing the letters on our sign at the end of our driveway. It was a Thursday, which meant Preacher was visiting members, visitors, and shut-ins. As I was finishing the sign, Preacher pulled into the driveway, rolled down his window, and motioned me over.

"You'll need to meet with William tonight and tell him about those text messages," he said.

"What! Why? You told me you would keep me in confidence," I respectfully replied. I was angry but knew better than to show it.

"I know I did, but William is thinking of moving to Florida with his family because of some health issues he's having. I told him that this wouldn't be a good time because he was under suspicion."

Now it all made sense. Preacher didn't want William to move, so he was going to threaten him with the information I had told him. Because Preacher believed that there was never a good reason to leave our church, he would do whatever it took to keep him around.

That evening I went out to eat with William. As I sat across the table from him, I explained how on the night Susan's water broke I had found text messages on her phone. When I finished, he explained how over the past year Susan had become obsessed with him, almost seeing him as a father figure. He went on to tell me several strange incidents that had happened recently— all because of Susan's unhealthy obsession with him. Not once did he admit to any wrongdoing. The next day I gave Preacher my report. Again, he seemed satisfied, and things went back to normal—at least for a while.

A few months after I confronted William, he called me. Before he even said a word, I could feel his anger over the phone. "Justin, my wife was just told by one of the girls in the church that I was under suspicion for being the father of Susan's child. I can only assume you are spreading these rumors since you stuck your nose in someone else's business. Buddy, so help me God, if I ever hear of you even breathing a word of what you found on that phone, and what you think that means, you. Will. Be. Sorry."

My hands trembled as I hung up the phone. I believed William. Only a year earlier, he had asked me to take part in throwing Susan's father a blanket party. William's friend had an unmarked van, and he told me he was planning on kidnapping Susan's dad, taking him out to the country, and beating the crap out of him. It never happened, but there was no doubt in my mind that William was not only willing but also capable of doing such a thing.

The next day, Preacher called me into his office. "Who else have you told about those text messages?" he inquired.

"Just a few people," I responded and gave him names.

"Justin, you had no business looking at Susan's phone. Telling other people about it was even worse."

"But Preacher, he's the father of—"

"*Justin!* You shouldn't have been looking on Susan's phone! William is very upset, and I don't blame him. What you're accusing him of is very serious. You're in trouble, and now you have to meet with the deacons."

The thought of meeting with the deacons terrified me. Far too often I had heard Preacher describe the monthly deacon meetings in our church staff meetings. It was never a good situation when you had to sit before those yes men for interrogation. Shame and guilt always followed, and those meetings rarely ended well.

The meeting was scheduled for the next Saturday. Before then, I made sure to call every person I had told about those text messages and apologize. I took the yellow folder I had stored under my mattress and burned it in my fireplace. It ended up that waiting for the meeting was worse than the meeting itself. But when I walked out of it, I made a vow to myself. I would never say another word about that situation again. In fact, if I tripped over Susan and William having sex, I would have apologized and taken it to the grave. When I left the church a few years later, rumors were still floating around the church about Susan and William, but I kept out of it.

* * *

In 2017, I got a call from Johnathan out of the blue. So much had happened during those thirteen years since the drama with Susan and William, including Preacher retiring and naming Johnathan his replacement. Johnathan had been to our church enough to make a significant impact on Preacher and the pulpit committee, a group of men designated to find Preacher's replacement. During our call, Johnathan got right to the point. He told me that the biggest reason he almost didn't take the position of senior pastor was that he would have to deal with the Susan situation. Many times he had brought up those text messages to the deacons, and every time they shut him down.

Because of a situation involving Susan's now twelve-year-old daughter, however, he was confronted with it once more.

"Justin, tell me again how you found those text messages and what they said. I just want to make sure I'm remembering everything correctly."

As if it had happened yesterday, I recalled in detail that night's events. When I finished, Johnathan asked me if I would be willing for him to use my name when dealing with this new situation. I agreed, and Johnathan hung up. I found out about a week later that after our phone call, he drove over to William's house. When he sat down in the living room—the same living room I had been watching movies in with William, Kelly, and Susan thirteen years earlier—Johnathan confronted William about Susan. William immediately and adamantly denied the affair and was upset that people were still spreading rumors all these years later. Then Johnathan told William he knew about those text messages. He explained that I had shown him the messages twelve years earlier and that William could lie about them all he wanted, but they both knew the truth.

At that point, William broke down and began to cry. He admitted everything—sending the text messages, being the father, and having an affair with Susan behind Kelly's back for the past thirteen years. Kelly was then brought into the room so William could confess to her. It turns out that Kelly had suspected something but chose to support and submit to William. To make matters worse, Kelly had all but estranged herself from her oldest daughter, who had also suspected what had happened. Over the years Susan and Kelly had become close friends, so Kelly disciplined her daughter for the way she treated Susan when Susan was at their house. In fact, Susan was so close to the family that when they moved to Florida during the winter months, Susan followed suit and moved there as well.

Obviously, when Kelly found out what had been going on under her nose for thirteen years, she was horrified and felt betrayed. But Kelly did what any wife attending a cultlike church like ours would do. She blamed herself.

Looking back, there was so much wrong with this situation, including me involving myself in something that was none of my business as well as the church involving itself. Yes, the church should have been a resource for Susan when she became pregnant, but the meetings, the level of detail they forced her to share, and the public humiliation they put her through was wrong, plain and simple.

* * *

By continually enforcing unsustainable rules that encouraged the forbidden, the church set itself up to turn a blind eye to adultery, men molesting their daughters, women molesting boys, incest, child pornography, child abuse, rape, and more. As a staff member, I was part of covering up and glossing over many situations that should have been exposed to the authorities; oftentimes, however, the only thing I felt like I could do was call the police to drop anonymous tips. Because I was fighting to endure my own abuse, both past and present, I was not in a place to truly help others. Preacher's abuse toward me only intensified, as did my desire to measure up to his impossible standards. Just when I thought things couldn't get worse, they did.

Chapter 10—The Last Days

My last two years at the church in 2008 and 2009 were full of the greatest psychological abuse I'd suffered yet. Joy's cancer was getting worse, so Preacher was under growing pressure to see God perform a miracle on her behalf. His verbal and mental abuse, which had extended beyond me to Jim and Pastor B, was so out of control that church members began noticing.

One day I was cleaning out the church's pole barn. On his way to run an errand, Preacher drove down the side road to check on my progress. After he put his car in park, he jumped out and began criticizing me for the way I was cleaning. "What do you think you're doing?" "Who told you to clean this way?" "You're so lazy!" and other insults spewed from his trembling lips. What Preacher didn't know was that another church member was inside the barn looking for a tool. While Preacher was yelling, this man stayed out of sight but heard every word. When Preacher left, this full-grown man emerged crying because of what he had just witnessed. Several other church members who overheard Preacher's mistreatment of me personally approached me to say they were praying for me.

Preacher became even more obsessed with women's dress, too. In our weekly meetings, he began outlining new dress standards that I was required to enforce with my choir—both on and off the platform. These standards included the length and style of women's hair, the color of their nail polish and makeup (skin tones that naturally complemented the skin, nothing that would contrast), and the size of purse they were allowed to carry. Preacher would provide examples of inappropriate attire by referencing a woman, usually a teenager, in the congregation.

One time, I was at church when a young teen girl walked past Preacher's office during an impromptu meeting on dress with some of the men in the congregation. Preacher called her in and had her bend over, bend down, sit down, stand up, and turn around so he could properly illustrate what not to wear. She walked out of his office in tears.

I began meeting weekly with the head deacon at his house to give him insight into how badly things were progressing with Preacher. Week after week, this dear deacon and his wife would sit in disbelief as I poured out my heart about all that had happened the week before. Week after week they would pray with me and for me. Week after week things only got worse, culminating with an incident right before Christmas in 2008.

I was working overtime seven days a week to get ready for our church's biggest event of the year, the Christmas cantata. Over seventy people were involved. I was especially excited this Christmas because a fellow musician and close friend offered to let me borrow all of his band's sound equipment and help me set it up. Also, a well-known photographer I had become friends with offered to take professional photos during the event.

The Sunday night before the dress rehearsal, I reinforced the dress standards to the choir, stressing that modest didn't equal frumpy. I mentioned that because we were using spotlights that year, the women should accentuate their makeup because the extra lighting would make them look washed out otherwise. This turned out to be pretty much the worst advice I could have given.

During our meeting that week, Preacher laid me out.

"I can't believe you would tell the women to wear extra makeup. You know how I feel about wearing too much makeup. What's your problem? All you care about is having a production, what with the lights and professional sound equipment. You even have a professional photographer coming. You have no spiritual insight. I don't even want to come to this thing because you've turned something sacred into something worldly."

I was crushed. I had poured my heart into this cantata. "Worldly" was the last thing on my mind. I had been praying for weeks for people to see Christ in the music and was beside myself knowing that Preacher thought I didn't care about the spiritual part. I called an emergency meeting with the head deacon and told him all that Preacher had said. He and his wife cried. We talked and prayed, just like we had done so many times before.

The cantata that Christmas turned out better than I could have ever expected. Everyone loved it except for Preacher. At the end of the night, one of the choir members got up in front of everyone and presented me with a gift bag that the choir had all chipped in for as a Christmas present. Inside was a card, a gift card, and chocolates. After I opened the gift and sat down, Preacher got up to give closing comments.

"Chocolate? Really? I think the last thing that Justin needs is chocolate," he said as soon as he reached the pulpit.

After that night, my love for directing music died.

Despite my history with abuse and extremism, 2009 was the worst year of my life. My love for directing the choir was one of the only things that had kept me going for the past five years. To make matters worse, my relationship with Megan was unraveling.

Megan was one of Pastor B's fourteen kids and one of my best friends. She was also the woman I had decided five years earlier that I wanted to spend the rest of my life with. The only problem was that Pastor B didn't feel the same way. He didn't mind us being friends. After all, we had grown up together and were like family. But when his oldest, unmarried, bitter daughter told her dad that our relationship was becoming romantic, he tried to stop it. At first he just tried to keep us from talking together at church, but when that didn't work, he took more extreme measures. For hours he would comb over his household's phone records to see if anyone in his family, from his wife down to his youngest daughter, had spoken with me. He also involved Preacher, who quickly determined that I had become both emotionally and mentally impure because I "liked" Megan and thought about her. Preacher reported my impurity to the deacons, and together they decided to put me on probation. "If I ever find out you guys have had any physical contact," threatened Preacher, "you will lose your job."

My biggest, darkest secret was that we had already had physical contact. We figured that we had already blown it by liking each other and thinking about each other, so why not "go all the way"? But we did not "go all the way." Not even close. But I knew even hand-holding would have gotten me fired, so Megan and I kept our relationship a tight secret. I should have either respected Pastor B's wishes and stayed away from Megan or faced him man to man to express my intentions and then move forward with the relationship. I didn't do the former because I didn't want to lose Megan, and I didn't do the latter because I didn't want to lose my job. Instead, we did our best to sneak around, and Pastor B did his best to catch us. He had thirteen other kids he should have been spending time with, but instead he became obsessed with our relationship. If he'd paid less attention to us, he might have stopped two of his other daughters from running away, two from contemplating suicide—one of whom attempted it—and one from being molested by her cousin.

In the summer of 2009, Megan and one of her sisters went to a camp a few states away to be counselors. All summer, Megan encouraged teens who had been hiding things from their parents to "unload their trucks." When she returned, Megan met with her dad and Preacher and unloaded her own truck about sneaking behind her dad's back with me—even though she was in her early twenties.

On a Wednesday morning in early August, Preacher called me into his office with Pastor B. He told me he knew everything about my relationship with Megan and that I too needed to come clean. I sat there not saying a word for what seemed like hours but was probably only ten minutes. I knew this was it. It was over. When Pastor B finally left the office, I told Preacher that I was officially resigning.

That night in church Preacher stood before the congregation and announced that I had resigned, calling it a "tragic situation." Over the next few days, I received several phone calls from choir members telling me they were praying for me. Some even came to my house, hugging me and crying. No one knew what the tragic situation was, so it was left up to their imaginations.

About a month later, Megan and I went before the church to apologize for sinning against them. Although it felt like it at the time, nobody forced me, a twenty-eight-year-old man, to place myself under Preacher's authority and publicly confess my sin. The Saturday before my confession, Preacher came to see me. He and the deacons had decided weeks ago not to go into detail regarding my relationship with Megan, saying only that it had been "inappropriate." But for whatever reason, Preacher changed his mind and decided he would preface my apology with details of our "steamy relationship," which consisted mostly of secret phone calls and hand-holding. He wanted to shame me in every way possible, and this was just another play out of his book. In desperation, I turned once again to the senior deacon for help. This time, Preacher was told by all the deacons to stand down. Regardless, I still felt indescribable shame apologizing before the church.

The rest of that year, I attended my home church as just a member. I learned a lot about myself as well as other people. Friends I considered closer than family turned into strangers overnight. I felt so ashamed every time I walked through the church doors that I left my glasses in the car so I wouldn't have to see people's faces. To avoid talking to anyone, I walked in during the opening prayer and left during the closing prayer. I also found out through friends that Megan and some of her family were spreading horrible rumors about our relationship that put me in the worst light possible. None of these rumors were true, but I was so broken at the time, I never bothered to combat them.

Because I was still going through the brokenness and repentance phase, I was not allowed to be involved in any ministry. I continued meeting semiregularly with Preacher for church discipline, but instead of desperately trying to prove myself to him in fear of losing my job, I just sat and listened as he taunted me with his opinions of the past six years as well as the present. Not defending myself while Preacher berated me brought about new accusations—I was hard and rebellious. Even though it hurt, I was too broken to defend the new abuse too.

When I resigned in August, we were right in the middle of planning the next Christmas cantata. About a week before the event, one of the choir members approached me about helping behind the scenes as a stagehand. My job would be to wear all black and switch out props when the lights were out. It took only a second for me to heartily answer yes. My choir had always worked hard for me; how could I not do the same in return? Of course, it would have to be approved by Preacher. A few days later, I was told by the same choir member Preacher didn't feel I was ready to be a nobody behind the scenes quite yet.

Despite the continued disappointments, I experienced a peace that I hadn't known for six years. In the months leading up to my resignation, I felt like I was starting to lose it mentally and emotionally. I would get so worked up that I would become physically sick. There were times I would wake up shaking in the middle of the night convinced that I was going to be fired the next day. When that happened, sometimes I would drive past the church or Preacher's house to see if I could spot something out of the ordinary that would tell me if I was going to get fired. Other times I would call my parents, waking them from a deep sleep to talk about getting fired. And I was insecure in my relationship with Megan, always thinking she was going to break up with me. Now, I no longer had to worry about losing my job or Megan.

Something strange happened also—I started receiving job offers from all over the country, which got me thinking that maybe Preacher was exaggerating when he told me I would never find a job anywhere else.

I welcomed 2010 by myself at home, but that was okay. I had a lot of decisions to make. I was looking into going back to school and considering some of the job offers I'd received. The one that stood out most was in Denver, Colorado. Shannon and her husband lived only miles away in Littleton, and while I was visiting them early that year, I became interested in getting a job with the Denver Police Department—one of the few decent jobs I could find that didn't require a degree from a real college.

On February 15, 2010, I left my home with my belongings and drove out to Denver. Before I left, I stopped by Preacher's house to say bye to him and Joy, whose cancer had spread to the point she was put on hospice. She woke up just long enough to say goodbye. Preacher stayed right by her side, tending to her every need. Along with Joy's entire family, Preacher was convinced God was going to heal Joy and bring revival to America through her recovery. That was the last time I saw Joy alive. A few weeks later, she passed away.

The eighteen-hour car ride to Colorado gave me plenty of time to think. *Will I ever return to my hometown? Will I ever be in the ministry again? Will I even make it as a police officer? Will I ever get married and have a family?* I had never experienced so many emotions at the same time. I was excited and scared, anxious and at peace, sad and happy. Before me was a brand-new chapter in my life. I didn't have any set plans for the future. All I knew is that I was driving to Colorado and when I got there, I would be staying for free in the garage of some man who attended my sister's church. I had no idea how much this man and his garage would change my life.

Chapter 11—Emily

I stood at the doorway of my room in the garage and stared in disbelief. What had been described to me as a place to stay was more like a five-star resort. The room had hardwood floors, plush furniture, a kitchenette, and a plasma TV hanging above a gorgeous stone fireplace. The scenery out every window was equally breathtaking with lush, green lawns, water fountains, and flowers. Never in my life had I stayed somewhere so beautiful. But the most beautiful part of this whole experience was getting to know the hosts of this stunning property, Karlan and Angela Tucker.

After settling in my new place, I began preparing for my upcoming interviews and tests with the DPD. I exercised and studied daily, drove around Denver and its surrounding cities, and went on ride-alongs with a DPD officer who attended the same church as me. I nailed my physical fitness test and my first several interviews and was looking forward to a call back.

I was thrilled to be starting my life over. I had always wanted to be a police officer, and now that dream was just weeks away from becoming a reality. I was away from the abusive environment I had grown up in and was experiencing some healing just by being twelve hundred miles away. I was attending my sister's church and making what I thought were lifelong friends. Karlan and his family took me in as one of their own, and I spent every moment I could with them. The Tuckers were to me what Jill's family had been when I was a teenager. I was blessed and happy. But at the same time, I was hurting and confused.

Every day I tried to make sense of the past six years. What was it about me that Preacher hated? Was he right—was I lazy? No doubt Preacher and Pastor B had received a call from the DPD since I'd put my previous work experience on my resume. Is that why they hadn't called back yet? One of the things I struggled with most was coming to terms Preacher—someone I trusted, loved, and respected—being wrong. My emotional pendulum swung wide; some days I would become enraged recalling all the abuse, and other days I would blame myself for being rebellious and having a bad attitude.

And then there was Megan. We had always been taught that there was only one person in the world for us to marry according to God's will. Was she the one? Did I blow it with her? Or did I miss God's will for me to marry another girl because I thought she was the one? Even across the country, I wanted everyone back home to know how successful I was in Colorado, partly because I wanted their approval, but mostly because I wanted Preacher, Pastor B, and everyone else who doubted me to know they were wrong. These all-consuming thoughts and desires kept me living in the past, even though my future was bright.

About a month after I arrived in Colorado, Karlan asked me if I wanted to make some money. I hadn't been hired on with the police department yet, so I immediately said yes. Karlan pulled a stack of cash from his pocket and peeled off several twenties and fifties. "Here you go," he said as he handed me the money. "I want you to take my cars to the car wash and have them all detailed. Keep track of your hours and the costs, and give me the receipts. I'll pay you twenty dollars an hour. If you're looking for more work after you wash the cars, let me know. There's plenty to do around here."

I almost fell over—$20 an hour? I quickly did the math. If I worked fifty hours a week, I would make $1,000 a week or

$50,000 a year, and I wasn't even paying rent. As a music pastor, I made around $24,000 a year. My take-home pay was $364 per week—$300 of which I turned over to my dad for house and utility payments before moving out. The remaining $64 was mine to keep for food, gas, and other expenses. After the month I spent watching videos and eating pizza the summer I graduated, movies and ordering out had become almost a daily tradition. I would quickly blow through that $64 by the middle of the week and then use a credit card or debit card to get through the rest of the week, quickly accumulating overdraft and late fees. I was financially irresponsible, but I just wanted to escape my life and feel normal.

My hands trembled as I grabbed the key to the first of six cars, all of which were expensive. All I could say to myself was, "You better not mess this up. You blew it at your last job; don't do it again." I took each car to the car wash and meticulously went over them to make sure they were immaculate on the inside and out. When I finished, I wrote down to the minute how long it took me to get those cars washed and to the penny how much it cost. When I turned everything over to Karlan, he paid me and asked if I was up to doing more work, to which I again quickly replied, "Yes!"

Over the next several months, I became Karlan's trusted right-hand man, saying yes to whatever he asked. If I didn't know how to do something, I learned. One time he asked me if I could help him build a presentation on his Apple computer using a program I had never even heard of. Without thinking I said yes and spent the rest of the day learning that program before building him an amazing presentation. Every time I completed a job, Karlan complimented and thanked me— something Preacher had never done, not even once. Every time Karlan praised me, I was determined to outdo myself on the next job. It felt so good to be working for a man who appreciated me. It also felt good to get paid at the end of each week.

In June 2010, a year after Preacher refused to let me off for Father's Day, I flew home to surprise my parents. I showed up in a stretch Hummer limo and took them out to dinner. I bought my dad a GPS for Father's Day and my mom the most expensive knife I could find at Williams Sonoma for her birthday. To be able to honor my parents in that way felt satisfying, but the feeling didn't last long. Every time I did something normal that I hadn't been able to do before, it confirmed how abnormal my upbringing was, which made me angry.

By that point, I had joined my sister's church. The night I became a member, the senior pastor stood up and said, "Now, I want everyone to welcome Justin and let him know how much we are glad to have him here. Also, Justin needs to find a good wife, so if you have suggestions, let him know." By the end of the next week, I had a list of fourteen eligible women, with no idea how to proceed. Here I was, twenty-nine years old and had never been on a normal date in my entire life. The closest I ever came was with Jill, but even then we had to travel two or three towns over to avoid being caught by my parents or nosy church members. I never actually dated Megan, and the girl I courted in college had to drive a separate car everywhere we went since driving together would have required a chaperone. When we walked together in public places, my potential helpmeet would order me to look down whenever she detected some type of immodesty, like a woman in worldly clothing. When we went out to eat, she sat on the same side of the booth as me to make sure I wasn't looking at other women.

So I did the only thing I could think of: I started at the top of the list and arranged to meet each woman. Some were easy to cross off because they were divorced or weren't Baptists. I did my best to get to know some of the other girls but eventually scared most of them away once they knew my intentions. I would have been scared away too if after only the third or fourth time I had ever talked to someone they were already interviewing me to be their spouse. I didn't understand the concept of "just friends," and even though these girls knew I had been given their names, they weren't ready to move from "hello" to "I do" that quickly.

Despite the fact that she had maligned my character with her false rumors, I still thought there was a chance something might happen between Megan and me. I was getting weekly updates from friends that made it clear she still had feelings for me. One day while I was working through my list of "prospects," I worked up the courage to text her. Megan's response indicated that my friends were very mistaken or that she was lying. Either way, I put that thought out of my mind and moved on literally within minutes.

When I worked as the music pastor, two women seemed to make it their life's mission to get me married to someone who was not Megan. Sometimes they even went so far as to contact the girl's father for approval, and all I had to do was pretty much sign on the dotted line to close the deal. Now that I was in Colorado and ready to move on, I contacted some of these girls again and their parents and pastors. Without exception, I was turned down almost immediately, realizing my reputation in any of my former circles had been destroyed. I wasn't surprised. Growing up, my friends and I had ruined people's reputations countless times just because we didn't like them. Our church was small, but the circles of gossip were big. When I became the music pastor, we used to discuss in staff meetings the most effective ways to ruin a member's reputation if they weren't doing what we thought they should be doing. Even though I didn't really participate in the maligning and backbiting, I didn't do anything to stop it either. We played dirty and dishonest and spread a lot of lies. No doubt I was reaping what I sowed.

After about a month of trying to find "the one" at my new church in Colorado, I gave up. I decided that I would rather remain single than marry the wrong woman or someone I wasn't attracted to because it was "God's will" for us to be together.

By the fall of 2010, I was on the verge of accepting a job with the Denver sheriff's department. I hadn't gotten an offer from the DPD yet, so I applied for a position with the sheriff's office. While I was waiting to hear back, Karlan offered me a job at his company. Even though I had always wanted to work in law enforcement, I had grown to love and respect Karlan and couldn't think of a better man to work for, so I decided to take his offer. The day I started, Karlan told me Zig Ziglar's railroad story:

In the 1950s, an incident took place on a sweltering summer afternoon alongside a railroad track where a crew of workers was doing some repair work. A train came chugging down the track and pulled off on a side rail. A window opened and a voice—a man's voice—shouted out, "Dave! Dave Anderson, is that you?"

It was; in fact, Dave Anderson was in charge of the crew. "Yeah, Tim, it's me," he shouted back.

The man on the train, Tim Murphy, yelled out, "Well, come on over here and let's chat a while."

So Dave stopped what he'd been doing and joined Tim Murphy in his private air-conditioned railroad car for almost an hour, no doubt happy to get out of the broiling sun. When the conversation ended, he made his way back to his crew working on the track. The flabbergasted crew stared at him in utter shock and said something to the effect of, "That was Tim Murphy, the president of the railroad."

"Yup, it sure was," Anderson said.

They all gathered around and excitedly wanted to know how Dave knew Tim Murphy, the president of the railroad, for God's sake, to say nothing about how he got to be such good buddies with the man and on a first-name basis to boot!

Dave explained: "Well, it's quite simple—when I started with the railroad over twenty years ago, Tim Murphy started at the same time; we've been pals ever since."

Now the crew is astonished as much as they are confused. They want to know how it is that Dave and Tim Murphy started working for the railroad at the same time, and Murphy rose to such dizzying heights while old Dave is still working on the track in the hot sun. How in God's name did that happen?

Dave looked wistfully up into the sky and said, "A little over twenty years ago Tim Murphy went to work for the railroad; I went to work for $1.75 an hour."

Karlan followed up his story with this piece of advice: "Justin, there is no glass ceiling here if you work for the railroad. Find ways to improve yourself as well as the company, and there are no limits to where you can go."

* * *

In early October 2010, I got a call from one of Megan's sisters, Donna. Donna and her new husband, Bob, were living on the East Coast and were on the "outs" with her family and our home church because she married Bob against her parents' and

Preacher's permission. Donna was calling to tell me about a girl she had heard about who was mutual friends with some of my Facebook friends. "Her name is Emily, but that's all I know about her," she told me. Out of curiosity, I went to Facebook and searched for the Emily who was mutual friends with some of mine. There were several, but only one took my breath away. Hoping this was the Emily Donna had been talking about, I requested her friendship.

A few days later, Emily accepted. After about a week, she asked me on Facebook how I knew our mutual friends. I would find out later that Emily was pretty creeped out that I'd requested her friendship but didn't contact her after that. But I still didn't know how to play this dating game. I sent Emily a private message and asked her several questions, hoping she would write back. A few days later I received her reply, but nothing else. She didn't make it easy for me to write back, but I did.

Over the next several weeks, Emily and I Facebook messaged each other regularly. We had a lot in common, and writing her was my favorite thing to do after work at night. After a while, we began instant messaging each other and often welcomed in the next day together because we lost track of time. In early November, I asked Emily for her phone number, and we began texting throughout the day. By this time I was beginning to get suspicious since she hadn't called. Emily was twenty-six and beautiful, and we had so much in common. Her writing and grammar was impeccable, and she seemed to really like communicating with me. So I began wondering if she had a speech impediment or a high-pitched voice, or maybe a very low voice. My dad started teasing me about it, and even though I would laugh along, I was dying to hear her voice.

I don't remember what excuse I came up with to call Emily, but I'll never forget hearing her sweet voice for the first time. I remember exactly where I was and exactly what we talked about. After that, we spoke every day. By late November, things were getting a little more serious with Emily. She had been planning a trip out to Colorado to visit some mutual friends, and we decided that I would fly out to her house in Illinois several days before so I could meet her family and then fly back to Colorado and spend time with her there.

I was now in uncharted territory. It still seemed too good to be true, so was it? When I saw Emily for the first time, were we going to shake hands? Hug? I couldn't help thinking about what I had been taught—holding hands leads to kissing, which leads to sex, which leads to dancing! Oh, how I desperately wanted to be able to say on my wedding day that we had never danced.

Then there was the matter of asking for her parents' permission. Was I supposed to call her parents now, or wait till I saw them in person? I was twenty-nine and Em was twenty-seven, so did I even need to ask her dad for permission, or just his blessing? But the biggest concern weighing on me was what Em would say when she found out about Carol Lynn and Megan. So I decided to tell her before I met her in person. I was already falling hard, and I knew when she found out about my past, she might call it off. In that case, I just wanted to get it over with.

To my surprise, when I told her about Carol Lynn, Emily became outraged, but not with me. "Why isn't that woman in jail? Why didn't your church or family turn her in? Did you ever get any counseling?" Then she said, "Justin, I'm so sorry that happened to you." Even though I tried to tell her it was my fault, this was first time anyone had ever reacted like this to my past abuse.

When I told her about Megan and having to confess our "sins" before the church, she literally laughed out loud because she thought I was joking. Emily had grown up in similar cult-minded circles, but even this was over the top to her.

With my two confessions out of the way, I began to make plans with Emily for our time together. We decided that to make things as uncomplicated as possible, we would not have any physical contact for the time being except for hello and goodbye hugs. My cult-minded church had taught me that it's impossible for young adults to have self-control, which is why chaperones are necessary. They taught me to live by the six-inch rule. They taught me that even holding hands would lead us down a road we would wish we hadn't gone down. They told countless stories of couples who kissed before they were married and how it destroyed their marriages. They told stories of couples who never touched before they were married—not even to put the engagement ring on—and how they had the best marriages.

Emily and I established our own boundaries from the time we met face to face till she walked down the aisle and never once strayed from them. We don't have one regret about our premarriage relationship. Actually, that's not true—Emily and I both wish we had dancing at our wedding.

* * *

By Christmas 2010, I had decided after spending just a few hours with Emily in person that I wanted to spend every moment of the rest of my life with her. With other girls I had attempted to date or court, my test for their potential as a wife was to ask, "Could I live with her?" A lot of times the answer was yes, but with Emily, the answer was, "I can't live without her."

On March 17, 2010, I proposed to Emily. From the moment I had to say bye at the airport after Christmas, I had begun planning it. I purposely chose St. Patrick's Day because of my distant Irish heritage. For weeks leading up to our engagement, the only time I would Skype with Emily was when I was sitting on a certain chair with the same blanket draped over it, with a picture on the wall behind me. I was sharing an apartment with a roommate by then, so I sent my dad a chip of paint from my wall, which he had matched at Home Depot and then used the paint on a four-by-four piece of drywall. When I flew to Illinois to propose, I took the blanket and photo on the wall. My parents and friend met me at the hotel and quickly helped me replicate the background Emily was used to seeing. Then I called her to begin our St. Patrick's Day Skype date we had been planning for weeks.

"I have a surprise for you," I told Emily. "I found a restaurant not far from you that serves authentic Irish food and ordered you a meal. All you have to do is pick it up." We hung up and I texed Em the directions, then rushed off to the nearby park and called her on her cell. "I need you to do one more thing before you pick up your food. There's a park nearby, and I need you to throw a rock into the river there and make a wish. There is an old Irish tradition that says on St. Patrick's Day if you throw a stone into the river and make a wish, it will come true."

Still on the phone, I anxiously watched as Emily drove into the parking lot of the park, walked toward the river, picked up a rock, and threw it inside.

"Did your wish come true?" I asked over the phone while walking toward her from behind.

"No," she said.

"Well, what did you wish for?"

"I wished that you were here right now, but I already know you are in Colorado."

"Are you sure?" I was now close enough where she could hear me both over the phone and faintly in person. She turned around at my voice. I had been planning for weeks what I was going to say at that moment, but it was under the assumption that Emily was going to be speechless and that I would have the floor. I hadn't planned for what was about to happen.

"What? How? Where? How did you get here? You were just in Colorado. I saw you there. How long have you been here? How long are you staying? Why didn't you tell me you were coming? Does my family know you're here? Is your name really Justin?"

At that point, I became speechless and muttered something about how I loved her and would be honored to spend the rest of my life with her, and would she marry me?

"Yes!" she shouted. "Yes, yes, yes!"

It was the happiest day of my life.

Chapter 12—Starting Over

The spring of 2011 should have been the happiest time of my life. I was newly engaged to my best friend and the love of my life, and we were planning our wedding and honeymoon together. We had enrolled in scuba diving classes—a lifelong dream of mine—so we could dive on our honeymoon. I was killing it in my new job. And Emily would be moving to Colorado in just a few weeks so we could more easily plan our future together. Life was the best it had ever been. But instead of being happy, I was angry, bitter, and miserable.

A few weeks prior I had watched a *20/20* special called "Independent Fundamental Baptist Cults." I sat there speechless as I listened to story after story of teens being sexually molested by predators in the churches they attended—teachers, pastors, and sometimes even fathers. When the churches found out, the leadership covered up the abuse, blaming and punishing the victims instead. Names of pastors and evangelists whose preaching I had sat under and names of churches I had attended flashed on the screen. I felt my face turn red as the reality of my past began to hit me. It had been twelve years since everything had happened with Carol Lynn, and for the most part, I thought I had dealt with it all. Now, as I was watching this special, I realized for the first time that I could have been part of that investigation. *20/20* should have been filming my church and holding my pastor accountable. I had never felt so many emotions at one time—anger, hurt, confusion, bitterness, insecurity, and devastation.

The next Sunday, I intentionally missed church for probably the first time in my life. I wasn't sick, out of town, or too busy—

just furious. I called my parents the next week and lashed out at them for their part in not putting Carol Lynn behind bars. After work at night, I began researching lawyers and the statute of limitations for criminal sexual conduct. When I realized that the statute of limitations had passed, my anger deepened.

And then I received a Facebook message from Carol Lynn.

Congratulations! She is a very beautiful woman and you both look crazy happy. I pray God's blessings on your life together and am happy for you both!

I could only see red. My heart was pounding so hard it was almost pulsing visibly through my shirt. I hadn't seen or been forced to interact with Carol Lynn since I had moved to Colorado. But now, all I could think of was a phone conversation I had had with her twelve years earlier, when she had burst into tears and told me she couldn't imagine me marrying some other girl, that she would be weeping in the congregation during my ceremony.

I quickly wrote back the meanest and most hateful message I could think of:

You are a pig, and should never contact me again. Watch the 20/20 special that aired last Friday about adults who do sick things to children that are under the age of consent. I will be blocking you on FB after I send this message so don't bother responding. Leave me alone or so help me God, I will blow this wide open!

For the next several months, I barely attended church. When I did go to church, I hated it. I quit exercising and began eating excessively. I was already overweight, but now I'd become obese. My bitterness toward Carol Lynn grew, as did my bitterness and hatred toward Preacher and anyone else involved in that situation. Being with Emily helped bring a little healing, but experiencing how good and loving she was also shed light on how abusive the past twelve years had really been.

* * *

It was time to start sending out wedding invitations. Emily invited more guests than I did, but I made a small list of family and friends and sent it to my parents, who had agreed to pass out the invitations at church. My mom called me the day the list arrived and asked if I intentionally left Preacher off. "Absolutely I did," I sneered. "I don't want him anywhere near my wedding, and neither does Emily." I felt pretty satisfied with my decision, but I knew clinging to bitterness and anger was only affecting me and was starting to affect Emily. When we attended church, I barely sang and was constantly on my phone. I couldn't even make it through the beginning of the service without getting angry at Preacher. I knew I should forgive him, but I felt my anger was justified, so I refused. I think Emily could tell I was upset but didn't know how to help.

A few weeks after sending my invitation list, I drove to Ogden, Utah, to support a friend running a marathon. On the way there and back, I listened to the audiobook *Unbroken* by Laura Hillenbrand, the amazing story of Louis Zamperini, an Olympian who joined the Air Force during World War II. His plane was shot down over the Pacific Ocean, and he spent forty-seven days at sea before being caught by the Japanese. Over the next several years, he suffered unimaginable abuse at the hands of his captors. When Louis returned to the States after the war, he suffered from PTSD, which drove away almost everyone he loved. After Louis became a Christian, he chose to forgive the men who tortured him unrelentingly, a decision that transformed his life.

I certainly did not buy that book with forgiveness in mind. Nonetheless, I was listening to this story of Louis's inner battle while fighting my own battle in my mind. For years while Louis was a POW, the Japanese controlled everything about him. And after the war, when he was thousands of miles away, they were still controlling him. He was isolated from his family as a POW, but when he returned, he was isolating himself from them voluntarily. When Louis chose to forgive his abusers, I was immediately humbled and convicted. What I had experienced, though devastating to me, wasn't even comparable to what Louis had been through. Yet just like him, I could see that twelve hundred miles away, I was letting my past control me to the point that I was miserable. I did not want to bring that baggage into my marriage.

As I drove through the mountains, I struggled with the decision to forgive Preacher, who had never asked for my forgiveness. About a month before I moved to Colorado, the head deacon called to let me know he had made great headway with Preacher regarding the psychological abuse he had put me through and that he was on the verge of an apology. The week after I spoke to the deacon, Preacher and I met for breakfast. In the middle of one of his berating sessions to me, he excused himself to use the restroom. When he returned, almost as if it were an afterthought, he said, "By the way, I just remembered,

I am sorry that I got frustrated with you for being so lazy, rebellious, and spoiled."

I remember feeling relieved that Preacher had admitted he had been frustrated with me. But now, as I was driving back from Utah, I kept remembering all the times he preached about how to biblically apologize—and his post-restroom apology was nothing like that. Then a message popped into my head that an evangelist friend of mine had preached on forgiveness. He had said that if you aren't willing to forgive someone, you should pray that God would make you willing to be willing. So I spoke out loud: "God, Preacher hurt me and I feel justified being angry, but it's destroying me. I am not willing to forgive Preacher, but I am willing to be made willing."

As God is my witness, the moment I finished, I had an overwhelming sense of peace. I wasn't angry or bitter anymore. I felt that a huge burden had been lifted off my shoulders. With God's help, I had experienced forgiveness, and it felt wonderful.

As soon as I got home, I called my parents and asked them to send a wedding invitation to Preacher in the mail. A few days later, before Preacher received my invitation, I checked my email and saw this:

Hi Justin,

I have wanted to call or email you for some time. I am not sure which is better. The phone seems to be more personal; however, I think that I could express myself more clearly through email. The Lord is continuing to do a work in my life. On Wednesday night, a week ago, I asked the church to forgive me. As the Lord has revealed to me over the last thirty years, I have enforced standards without life and love, 2 Corinthians

3:6: ". . . For the letter killeth but the Spirit giveth life." When people failed to meet the standard I became irritated with them. My response was worse than their fault. The beam needed to be removed from my eye so I could see clearly to remove the mote from their eye. I failed to love them as they were so I could be effective in helping them to become what God wanted them to be. I taught them "what" they should do without showing them "how" to get there through Christ and the exchanged life. I walked in truth without walking in love. I have done the same to you; I was hard on you and not loving. I am deeply sorry and ask your forgiveness. I pray for the Lord's blessing on your life, marriage, and ministry. May the Lord Jesus fill you with His life that it may overflow to others.

Love,
Preacher

* * *

A few months later in September, Emily and I were married. It was a great day, and our honeymoon was even better. We stayed our first night in a hotel room that had its own pool and hot tub. Then, for three days we rented a houseboat on the Illinois River. After that we spent a week in St. Lucia, diving at least two times a day. When we got back, Emily found a job at a local clothing store, and I continued to work for Karlan. I had recently gotten promoted and was busy "working for the railroad."

Shortly into our first month of marriage, Emily and I began experiencing problems. Emily didn't feel loved by me, and even though I did love her with all my heart, I was having intimacy issues. I first noticed it one day when I came home from work. The moment I walked through the door, Emily threw her arms around me and began kissing me. I immediately flashed back to the time Carol Lynn grabbed me and began kissing me for the first time. I began to panic and pushed her away. "Geez, let me get in the door before you go attacking me like that," I snapped. I saw the hurt in Emily's eyes, and even though I desperately wanted to explain how I felt, I thought it would hurt her even more by telling her that her initiating intimacy brought back terrible memories. So I came up with excuses instead.

These kinds of situations happened weekly, sometimes daily. I didn't mean to hurt Emily. In fact, there was no one on earth I loved more and wanted to hurt less. But I didn't know how to deal with the past or that our intimacy issues even had anything to do with it. But Emily knew it.

One day after I had turned her advances down yet again she said, "I hate what that woman did to you. I wish you would get counseling."

"I don't need counseling," I replied. Growing up, counseling typically meant two things—you were involved in some sin and needed to stop, or you were bitter or angry and needed to forgive. So instead of getting help, I turned once again to my poor eating habits. On Saturdays I would sleep in, eat an enormous breakfast and lunch, watch TV until I fell asleep on the couch, then wake up to take Emily out to dinner and stuff my face. On Sundays I would do the same while squeezing in church. On Mondays I would tell Emily we shouldn't eat out so much—maybe once a week at most. But on Monday night, we would go out to eat. In our first year of marriage, I gained 30 pounds, tipping the scale around 285. Some turn to alcohol to drown bad memories, others to drugs. But my addiction became food. And eventually it began affecting my health; I would get out of breath just walking to the car. Emily was worried about my weight gain, but she was always so kind and supportive. She never put me down or judged me.

Another way the past continued filtering into the present was through our views on church. We had recently gotten a new pastor, who was taking things in a different direction. One Sunday we noticed two projectors and screens in the sanctuary and sang a new song that wasn't a hymn. When we got home, I looked up the song on YouTube and was horrified. It was everything I had been warned about growing up—guys in jeans holding microphones, drums, the satanic rock beat. And even though none of that existed at church, the association alone was crossing a huge line.

Emily immediately wanted to leave the church. That was her family's go-to anytime they had issues with the church they attended. I, on the other hand, had never left a church in my life except to move across the country. So we decided to stay to see what would happen. I had always been taught that as soon as the music starts to slide, it would just be a matter of time before everything else did as well. And sure enough, not long after the pastor showed up in a suit coat and no tie. The week after that, the huge cross-bearing pulpit was replaced with a small podium—a sure sign that the pastor was trying to minimize the Gospel, according to my upbringing.

Another Sunday one of the ushers taking the offering was wearing a pair of dress slacks and a polo. I was beside myself. *After all God has done for you, how could you do any less than give Him your best?* I thought. *If he was going to visit the president, wouldn't he have worn a suit?* And women were beginning to wear dress slacks—even on the platform! Between that, the contemporary music, and the newly added guitar during song service, Emily and I decided to visit other churches. Emily was six months pregnant, and we wanted to make sure our church's values aligned with what we were going to be teaching our child.

The first church we visited was a very conservative Baptist church. I decided to wear nice jeans and a button-down shirt because a work friend told me he immediately felt judged by the "Christians" there for wearing jeans and a T-shirt. I assumed he wasn't feeling uncomfortable because of the Christians judging him but because he was experiencing the unmistakable conviction of the Holy Spirit. But now I wanted to test my theory.

I'll never forget walking through the doors of that church. A greeter was handing out bulletins and saying good morning to everyone as they walked inside. As we walked in, he said good morning to Emily, but when he turned to me, he seemed unable to speak and only handed me a bulletin. Then he turned to greet the person behind me. We sat near the front, and I sang out at the top of my lungs to the familiar songs. About halfway through the first song, though, I noticed everyone on the platform was staring at me with the most confused looks. I couldn't figure out why for a few minutes, but then it hit me—here I was, dressed like a non-Christian but singing like a Christian. I leaned over to Emily and told her to watch the leadership up there, and we both got a good laugh from their reactions. During the invitation, the pastor had everyone close their eyes and bow their heads. When he asked if anybody needed to get saved, I peeked. The pastor was looking directly at me to see if I would respond.

Emily and I decided that even though we didn't know what church we would land at, it certainly wouldn't be a church like that. Over the next few weeks, we visited two other churches and concluded that at least for the time being, we needed to stay at our current church. As long as the preaching was solid, we could overlook minor things like music and dress.

A few months later, our firstborn son, Jackson, came into our lives. I'll never forget when the doctors put Jackson into my arms for the first time. This overwhelming sense of protection came over me, where I would do literally anything to keep him from harm. I remember when a nurse came in for a test and pricked his heel with a needle. When he let out a little squeal, I wanted to put that nurse in a headlock—the poor woman was only doing her job. I had never felt that way before.

During the next several months, my abusive past came into a whole new light. Before Jackson was born, I struggled with the past—what to call it, how much of it was my fault, what I should have done differently. Now, as I held my helpless little man in my arms, I imagined him in the different situations I had faced—specifically the sexual abuse—and shuddered. I vowed to myself that I would do anything in my power to protect him from the same abuse I had experienced.

By the time our precious daughter, Juliette, was born fourteen months later, Emily and I had a completely different outlook on life. We now viewed everything through the "what would be best for our children" lens. This affected every area of our lives—what kind of car we drove, where we went out to eat, where we vacationed, where we lived, and if and when we slept. We were somewhat prepared for this new mindset since many who had gone before us warned us about it. What we weren't prepared for was how our perspective on church would change. Before having kids, all that mattered to us was that the preaching was solid and biblical. But especially because of my background, everybody suddenly became suspect to us, and as new parents, we no doubt overreacted in some situations. The safety of our children trumped everything, and there was no room for benefit of the doubt.

In May 2017, when our kids were still babies, we left our church. It was one of the hardest decisions I had ever made. I am thankful that I was able to meet with the pastor and that he supported our decision.

* * *

Cult-minded churches demand loyalty. In the church I grew up in, there was never a good reason to leave—even if you moved across country for a job, you were out of the will of God. So when we did leave our church, I was once again navigating uncharted territory. I didn't even know where to begin looking for a new church. I knew what kind of church we absolutely wouldn't attend—a cultish church, and there seemed to be plenty of them around. A close second were liberal, new evangelical, backsliding, rock-concert and non–King James Version watered-down-preaching churches I had been raised to avoid, and there seemed to be plenty of those around too. The thought of trying to find that balance was so overwhelming that we took a break and just enjoyed being together as a family for about a month. After that, we decided the best way to find a church would be for me to attend several churches in the area alone. If I liked a particular church, then Em would attend the next Sunday. If she liked it, then we would attend as a family.

The first church I scoped out was another Baptist church, the denomination I had been brought up in and was convinced was the only denomination God smiled upon. The pastor was at the door greeting people and shook my hand as I walked in. The members seemed so friendly, and I met several people that day. The song service wasn't rock and roll, and the pastor preached out of the good old KJV, but his sermon was different from any I had ever heard before. I left that service with more questions than answers. There was definitely a familiarity to the whole experience, but I couldn't quite put my finger on what was different. I had checked out the nursery, though, and felt comfortable enough to have Em attend the next Sunday.

Emily and I talked after we came home that Sunday. We both liked the church and were excited to bring our kids the following week and to schedule a meeting with the pastor. Maybe this whole finding a new church thing was a piece of cake! That Sunday we brought the whole family, and I set a time for the pastor to come over that following Tuesday. I preordered our favorite steaks from our local butcher, Em cleared her night of piano lessons, and we cleaned our house from top to bottom.

All during dinner we asked questions about the pastor, his family, the church, and the church's standards. The pastor gave balanced answers, especially compared to what I had been brought up believing. However, two of his answers gave me serious pause. When talking about dress, he mentioned that he was pretty laid back but did require a suit jacket for anyone on the platform. Then he made this statement: "Of course, when a lady dresses immodestly, my wife will take her aside and confront her because, you know, we don't need that at our church."

When I asked him about his stance on alcohol, he simply quoted Proverbs 20:1 from the KJV—"'Wine is a mocker, strong drink is raging: and whosoever is deceived thereby is not wise.'" Oh, how well I knew that verse. As a child, my family read one chapter of Proverbs every day. Since it has thirty-one chapters, we read that verse about once a month.

"What about all the positive references to wine in Proverbs and other New Testament passages?" I asked.

The pastor repeated, "'Wine is a mocker, strong drink is raging: and whosoever is deceived thereby is not wise.'"

"So are you saying it is a sin to consume any alcohol whatsoever?" I responded. Once again the pastor repeated the verse, which struck me as odd. I wasn't looking for this pastor to give me his blessing to drink; I wasn't much of a drinker anyway. I was simply looking for a balanced, biblical answer, not the same verse repeated three times.

At the end of the night as the pastor was getting ready to leave, he prayed. I don't remember much of his prayer, but I'll never forget when he said, "And Lord, please show Justin and Emily if it's Your will for them to attend our church. And if it's not Your will, please show them that as well. We certainly don't want them at our church if it's not Your will, although I believe it is."

Suddenly it hit me—this man was on a sales call. His prayer was a classic sales technique. He had spent the entire night convincing us that his church was the perfect fit for us, but at the very end, he threw in the final sales pitch. Because I was working closely with independent financial advisors all over the country, I had heard something similar in sales presentations I can't tell you how many times: "Well, Mr. John Doe, when we sit down, we'll have an honest conversation about your needs to determine if we're a good fit. If we are, then I'll tell you how I can help. If we're not, I'll tell you that as well. The last thing I want as a fiduciary is to work with someone who's not a good fit." I'd never heard one advisor tell a qualified client that they weren't a good fit, nor in my years of ministry did I ever hear a pastor tell a prospective member they weren't a good fit.

Before the pastor came over, Em and I were 95 percent sure we had found our church home. When the pastor left, I asked Emily where she stood, and she said she had a bad feeling. "What kind of a church has a pastor's wife confronting another woman for the way she's dressed?" she asked. I agreed, but we decided to attend once more to make our final decision.

That Sunday a special guest speaker, a Christian lawyer, preached on prayer. He was a rather large man, which struck me and Emily as odd since the senior pastor had taken such a strong stance on alcohol based on Proverbs—the same book that condemns gluttony five times.

The sermon, based on James 5's call to pray earnestly, had four points regarding what we had to do to have power in prayer:

1. Ask
2. Get fervent
3. Get clean
4. Persist

At the end of the sermon, the speaker pulled off one of the best rigged invitations I'd ever seen. It was impressive. He closed his message with a story about his bedridden mother with polio. He told us how as a child, he used to sit at the top of the stairs and listen to her pray for him. He described in detail how she would be in so much pain that right in the middle of her prayers she would scream out, "Oh, God! I can't breathe! I can't breathe, God! The pain is too much, God! God, be with my boy. Help him to serve you." By this time, there was barely a dry eye in the auditorium. With trembling voice, he ended his message with, "My mom couldn't dress herself, she couldn't cook, she couldn't clean or go grocery shopping. But oh, she could pray."

Then he asked us to bow our heads and close our eyes as he asked the following question: "If you want to have power in your prayers, please raise your hand." As you could probably guess, hands shot up all over the auditorium. He could have gotten the same response if he had asked, "Who doesn't want to die a painful death?" or "Who doesn't want to get stabbed in the eye?" The shotgun invitation was simple—if you raised your hand, come forward. "When the altar gets full, just kneel in the aisles. If the aisles get full, just kneel in your seats." Emily and I watched in amazement as the altar filled up, then the aisles. After a few minutes, we were some of the only people in the entire place still standing. And that, my friends, is how you rig an invitation:

1. Tell a tearjerker story at the very end of your message.
2. Ask a question you know everyone's going to respond yes to.
3. Cleverly suggest that if you aren't the first one out of your seat when the music starts, you might have to kneel in your seat.
4. Sit back and let the fun begin.

We never visited that church again.

* * *

A month later on a Sunday morning, I attended another church nearby. We hadn't been to church since the lawyer spoke. So I Googled "churches in my area" and decided to visit the closest one. With hardly any expectations, I drove a few minutes down the road and pulled into the parking lot of the large church. The first thing I noticed when I walked into the auditorium were the guitars and drum on the stage. I immediately felt uncomfortable, but I sat down anyway and waited for the service to begin. I'm not sure why I didn't walk out. Maybe I was curious or needed to officially be able to cross this church off my list. I think more than anything I wanted to see if this type of church I'd been warned against was yet another lie.

I struggled throughout the worship service. People all around me were raising their hands during the songs. *What show-offs,* I thought. The senior pastor wasn't there, so the family pastor, Jim, preached on prayer, using the Lord's Prayer as a model of how we should pray. It was the most balanced, biblical message on prayer I had ever heard. The difference between that message and the last message I had heard on prayer was like night and day. I couldn't wait to get home and tell Emily all about it. The next Sunday we went together, and the Sunday after that we attended as a family. We had finally found our home church.

Aside from the biblical preaching that had no agenda and no bias, there were several other reasons we chose this church. One of the biggest was the lack of judgment. I had never been in a church that didn't judge people for how they dressed, when they attended, how many kids they had, or what kind of car they drove. Unlike the church I grew up in, this church didn't conceal gossip by calling it "sharing prayer requests," nor did it judge by telling people "Thus saith the Lord" about a particular "sin." I was so convicted of how judgmental I had been all my life that one of my favorite parts of going to this church became the song service. Sometimes we even find ourselves raising our hands while singing—so far, no lightning bolts.

Another is the conviction of the Holy Spirit. In every other church I had attended, conviction was brought about by pastors and evangelists yelling and manipulating at us. These masters of conviction often had high numbers during their invitations. I myself used to become so overwhelmed that I would kneel at the altar to confess, but rarely did I change. That's because man-induced conviction doesn't last. At this church, the pastor preached God's Word and left the conviction up to the Holy Spirit. As it turns out, the Holy Spirit does a much better job.

This church also eased our worries about our kids being raised in a church with a safe, godly children's program. From the moment we dropped them off, Emily and I were both overwhelmed by the grace and kindness shown toward them. Jackson has speech apraxia as well as a sensory processing disorder, so he is often misunderstood, judged, and treated differently. Once in our previous church when Emily went to check on him, he was sitting by himself in a corner of the baby nursery crying while the two nursery workers were "sharing prayer requests," not paying attention to him at all. He was three at the time and supposed to be in another class, so Emily asked why he was in the nursery. She was told he was being disruptive during the last five minutes of the twenty-minute lesson.

At this church, Jackson was assigned a "buddy"—a teen or older adult who hung out with him the entire time to make sure he was doing okay. Also, the nursery security and safety protocols were the best we had ever seen. In fact, about a year after joining, Emily and I realized we had gotten so comfortable dropping our kids off at the nursery that we had become complacent. Even though the church was doing its part to protect children from predators, we knew we still needed to do our part. Ever since, we've tried to look at everything with fresh eyes because predators are so skilled in their craft they can easily fool everyone around them.

After settling in to our new church, I felt like I was discovering God for the first time. I was learning so much about who I was compared to who He was, and it was overwhelming and convicting at the same time. I also began realizing how cult-minded the church I grew up in really was. Emily and I began discussing regularly how different our lives were compared to even a few years earlier. And I began opening up to her about my past.

One day as we were talking, she said, "Honey, you should write a book. You were so sheltered growing up, but it sounds like you and your friends weren't protected at all." I loved the idea, but I didn't feel worthy at the time. After she made the recommendation, however, I began sharing my story with advisors I was working with all over the country. Without exception, they either had had similar experiences or knew someone who did. Emily's recommendation and my conversations with advisors gave me the motivation I needed to start writing my book. I could finally approach my past and therefore my book from a place of forgiveness. I could finally heal.

Conclusion—Forgiveness and Restoration

I sat at the desk in my hotel room staring at my computer screen. It was October 2018 and I had left home for a few days to work on my book, but now I felt paralyzed and couldn't write even one word. I finally gave up and, as I had done thousands of times before, went out to a restaurant and gorged on food.

When I began writing the book in early 2018, I knew there were at least two potential outcomes: infuriating a few hundred people or spreading awareness and possibly helping thousands to heal. I was forced to weigh the pros and cons of each.

Because I was writing about real-life experiences involving current and former church members, and because of the sensitive subject material, I knew my book would be highly controversial and that, no doubt, people would be infuriated. But my desire was never to call out individuals and places involved in this abuse. I also knew that much had changed at the church since I left, too. It came under new leadership that was doing its best to combat the cult-minded thinking that permeated for thirty-plus years. My former pastor seemed happily remarried and at peace based on photos I'd seen flashing across social media. And many others I was mentioning in my book I considered friends. For these reasons, I decided to take a careful approach and to be as nonspecific as possible. I knew I had a story to tell, despite the inherent risks.

So I made a promise to myself and before God that I wouldn't write my book from a place of bitterness or anger but rather from a place of forgiveness and healing. I regularly checked in with myself to make sure I had truly forgiven all from my past. But as I sat in my hotel room trying to write about the woman who took my innocence, I realized I had not forgiven her, nor did I have any intentions to do so. "She was a monster and incapable and undeserving of my forgiveness," I kept saying to myself over and over. I felt that forgiving my abuser was somehow admitting that what she did was okay. I had convinced myself that because I didn't consciously dwell on that part of my life every moment of every day, I didn't even need healing and forgiveness.

I also knew if I forgave this woman, I could no longer hate her with every part of my being. Hate didn't even begin to describe the emotions I felt. Several years before starting my book, Emily and I watched a movie in which once a year, there were no consequences for an entire day. After the movie Emily asked me what I would do if I had no consequences for a day. What came out of my mouth without even a moment's hesitation shocked us both. "I would fly home, cut Carol Lynn's throat, and watch her bleed out until she took her last breath." I loathed this woman, and it was affecting me in ways I didn't realize.

After I came back from eating, I sat back down and continued to write my book, skipping over the chapter about my sexual abuse. When I came home from my trip, I was consumed with my past. I now thought about my abuse every day. At night, I would have recurring nightmares about it. I gained even more weight. Almost all my clothes were too tight for me; I had outgrown all my belts, and I wore a sweater every day thinking it would somehow disguise how obese I had become. I refused to buy clothes my size because I planned on starting my diet again "tomorrow." I developed sleep apnea as a result of my weight gain and got out of breath walking down the stairs. I could barely play with my kids. I hated myself and my body and wanted so badly to lose the weight, but I couldn't.

In November 2018, about a week before my birthday, everything came to a head. I was so tired, partly from my nightmares, partly from how unhealthy I had become. I was miserable because of my sheer hatred for Carol Lynn. Every morning I would wake up and ask myself if I would still kill her if there were no consequences, and every morning the answer would be yes. I knew I had to forgive but couldn't bring myself to do so.

As I continued writing, I began reflecting on how life changing forgiving Preacher was. But I had my doubts that the same God who helped me forgive Preacher could help me forgive Carol Lynn. After all, deep down Preacher had good intentions. He certainly wasn't a predator, and though it seemed so at times, he was not a monster like Carol Lynn. Regardless, out of desperation I found myself once again crying out, "God, I'm not willing to forgive Carol Lynn. I don't even know what that would look like or where to begin. But my bitterness and anger is destroying me and my family, and I don't want it to any longer. So even though I'm not willing to forgive, I'm willing to be made willing."

I went to bed that night not thinking much about what I had prayed. In the morning, I asked myself that same question about killing her if there were no consequences—and the answer was a definite no. In fact, I couldn't even finish the question in my mind. For the first time in twenty years, I no longer had even once ounce of hatred toward my abuser.

It was a strange feeling having that weight lifted off my shoulder. I thought the only result would be better sleep and deeper happiness, but I was never more thankful to be wrong. I first noticed changes during the week of my birthday. Every year for the past twenty years, I would use my birthday week as an excuse to binge, promising I'd start my diet later. But on the first night of this birthday week when Emily asked me where I wanted to eat for dinner, I said, "Let's just eat in tonight."

Emily looked at me, her eyes filled with genuine concern, and said, "Jay, are you feeling okay? Is everything all right?"

"I think so. I just don't feel the need to stuff my face." The next night the same thing happened, and the next, and the next. When Emily took me out on my birthday, I just ate a normal-sized meal. I continued this new habit of moderation and lost twenty pounds by Christmas. Today, I have lost over sixty pounds and counting.

Control over my eating was not the only thing that changed. For the first time since I had moved out on my own, I began putting my clothes away when I came home instead of throwing them on the bedroom floor. My car was cleaner. My interactions between people improved. Only months earlier, I hated speaking in front of my peers because I didn't think I had anything important to say. Now, I spoke my thoughts freely and fluidly. Whereas before I was afraid of confrontation, now I embraced it under the right circumstances. I was no longer concerned with how people viewed me or what they thought of me.

When my abuser took what wasn't hers twenty years ago, my self-hatred began manifesting itself through the way I ate, the clothes I wore, and ultimately my lifestyle. When Preacher abused me and my peers disrespected me, I just took it because I thought I deserved it. Oh, I would convince myself that I was turning the other cheek, but deep down I knew the truth. I wasn't worthy of anything but disrespect. Author and theologian Lewis Smedes said that when you forgive a wrongdoer, "you set a prisoner free, but you discover that the real prisoner was yourself." By not forgiving, I was a prisoner to food, to unhealthy relationships, to destructive patterns of behavior. When I forgave, I was set free; I was no longer a prisoner.

Even though I was thankful for looser clothes and a clean room, the change that has made the most impact in my life and has been the most rewarding has been in my relationship with Emily. From the moment I laid eyes on Em and decided I wanted to spend the rest of my life with her, my desire to love, cherish, and honor her began to grow. Despite all my issues, Emily gently encouraged me and loved me unconditionally. If I wanted to eat out, she would offer to drive. If I wanted to sleep all day on Saturdays, she would stay with me and read a book or check her email. When someone would insult me, she would want to tear them apart but supported my decision to turn the other cheek.

When we were first married, on two occasions Emily and I were approached by two different men we had never met. "Excuse me," they said to me, "is this your wife?" When I replied yes, they said, "Can I ask you how you did it? Your wife is gorgeous! She looks like a celebrity, but you . . . you are . . . well, you are *you*." Both times I smiled and said thank you since they had complimented my wife, but Emily was furious. "How could you let them insult you like that?" Today, I would agree with her position, but I had no self-respect then. I did not make life easy for Emily during those first several years, and I had a lot of healing to do.

About a month after I forgave my abuser, Emily and I were out on a date and she told me that for the first time since we had been married, she *consistently* felt that I loved her. I no longer pushed her away when she initiated contact. I no longer had flashbacks of Carol Lynn during our most intimate times.

I was free. I knew it, and so did Emily—and it has changed our lives.

A Note from the Author—My Why

When I was writing *Sheltered but Not Protected*, I often got asked, "Justin, why are you writing this book? Are you angry? Are you bitter? Are you just trying to air other people's dirty laundry?" Both the interrogations and accusations were plentiful. My salvation has been questioned. I've been accused of fighting against God and His church. I've been threatened with legal action. I've lost friends and family members and have been misunderstood by countless others. I've questioned my own ability to share my story in such a public way, too—I'm not a counselor, nor do I feel like I'm qualified to write a book. There have been times when I've even questioned in my own soul why I dedicated the past two years to putting my story and thoughts down on paper.

But the answer I always arrive at is this: If I can help just one person experience healing and forgiveness by becoming vulnerable and telling my story, then that is my why. If by sharing my experience I can startle someone into thinking twice about attending a cult-minded church, or letting their child sit on a close friend's lap or spend the night at a relative's house, then that is my why. If someone addicted to drugs, alcohol, food, or any other vice can see similarities in their own life and get the help they desperately need, then that is my why. If my two precious children can grow up in a world that is just a tiny bit safer as a result of my efforts to spread awareness of sexual abuse and its prevalence in unchecked religious organizations, then that is my why.

Some call it bravery, others call it stupid. Regardless of what "it" is, until I take my last breath, I will continue to call out and spread awareness about cultish churches that control their members by manipulation and intimidation. Churches and pastors that care more about their own reputations than about protecting victims from abuse. Churches and pastors that so grossly abuse the first amendment that they operate as if they are above the law. Let me be clear—not all churches fall into this category. In fact, I would say most churches don't. But there are plenty that do.

Awareness, forgiveness, and healing—that is my why.

When it comes to forgiveness and healing, here is some advice I wish I had known five, ten, fifteen, and twenty years ago that would have changed my life.

Get away from your abusive environment.

Taking that first step of getting away is often the hardest, which is one of the reasons abuse is so prevalent. Spouses are afraid to leave their abusive spouses, members are afraid to leave their abusive churches, children oftentimes don't even have a choice to leave their abusers. Nothing good can come from staying in an abusive relationship. Will he or she promise to change if you stay? Absolutely. Can he or she change? Maybe. Will staying help them change? Absolutely not. Besides, leaving your abusive environment isn't for the abuser, it's for you!

I realize it's easier said than done—I was in an abusive situation with Carol Lynn for almost a year as a teenager. I stayed in an abusive environment for six years when working at the church, and even then, I wouldn't have left if I hadn't been practically forced out. And that was just my job! I can't imagine what it would be like in an abusive marriage or family. My heart breaks at the thought of it. But for your own sake, get out! That might mean simply leaving your church. Guess what, regardless of how you've been brainwashed all these years, God is not going to punish you for leaving your church to protect yourself or your family. Getting away from your abusive environment might mean not going to visit your parents' for Christmas because your dad constantly belittles you or your wife—or worse, your kids. The applications are endless, but know this—a wound can't begin to heal if it keeps getting opened up. You can't begin to heal if you keep being abused.

Get proper counseling.

I mentioned that I didn't receive counseling for my abuse. That word wasn't even on my parents' or pastor's radar. For twenty years I struggled with pain and addiction I didn't even know was related to my abuse. I destroyed my body, ruined relationships, hurt the ones I love the most, and missed out on countless opportunities because of my extreme insecurity and lack of self-respect. I can't help but think that if I had gotten counseling from the right person, I could have avoided so much heart ache. If you are or have been a victim of abuse, please consider counseling.

I can't stress enough the importance of the right kind of counseling. There are many "counselors" out there who claim to be certified and qualified but are neither and can therefore cause irreparable damage. Sadly, some of them call themselves Christians and no doubt took a class in college that spoke about counseling. I've sat under these so-called counselors, and they are poison. They will encourage you to forgive your abuser without holding them accountable. They will make you feel worse about not forgiving than about your abuser abusing you. They will encourage a nice "sit-down" with your abuser to talk things out. They will often seem to take the side of the abuser and victim-shame. They will tell you, "Don't leave your husband," "Don't report your abuse," "Don't leave your church." That kind of counsel only made things worse.

Above all else, forgive- in your own time, and in your own way. "Forgiv[e] one another, as God in Christ forgave you" (Ephesians 4:32).

I can't stress enough the in your own time and way part to this. You should never be forced to forgive, or made to feel guilty or a lesser of a person for how you go about forgiving. When I first realized I hadn't forgiven my abuser, I couldn't wrap my head around it. I viewed my sexual abuser as an inanimate object that couldn't or didn't deserve forgiveness; it would be like forgiving a rock that had fallen on my head. As a husband and father, I couldn't fathom how my abuser could do what she did to me as a minor. Because I couldn't humanize her, she didn't deserve forgiveness. But I couldn't move on with my book until I knew that deep down in my heart, I had forgiven everyone. Knowing that I needed to forgive but not knowing how drove me to countless hours of study and research. I already knew what the Bible said about forgiveness—or at least what I grew up being told that the Bible said:

- **Forgive and forget (Psalm 103:12).** My church taught that since God put our sins as far as the east is from the west and will remember them no more—so should you.

- **He who is without sin cast the first stone (John 8:7).** God didn't punish the woman caught in adultery;

therefore, we shouldn't punish those who have wronged us. Leadership occasionally used this argument after they were sure a church member had repented and been restored. Repentance and restoration included a *lot* of punishment by the leadership, but once they determined a member had successfully graduated from the restoration process, how *dare* you suggest that person is anything but right with God—"if you're so perfect, cast the first stone."

- **Turn the other cheek (Matthew 5:39).** This verse, which suggests that if someone slaps you across the face, turn your head so he can slap you again, was used to advocate not holding someone accountable.

The misinterpretation and misuse of these verses' principles—and many more—had shaped my thoughts on forgiveness. If forgetting was part of forgiveness, then I was doomed. If forgiveness meant turning the other cheek and letting myself get abused, then I would die before forgiving. If forgiveness meant reconciliation, then there wasn't a chance I was going to forgive. And none of this takes into account that Carol Lynn never once reached out to apologize.

Sometime during the writing of this book, a friend shared an article called "What Forgiving an Abuser Doesn't Mean." In her article, Ashley Easter dispels ten myths regarding forgiving your abuser—and she should know considering she was raised in a cult-minded, abusive environment like mine. This is one of the best, most balanced lists I've ever seen on the topic:

1. **Forgiveness does not mean the abuser must be involved.** Sometimes the abuser does not apologize,

sometimes the abuser is no longer living, and sometimes it is not healthy to have contact with the abuser. Even if the abuser is truly sorry and openly repents, forgiveness is about your healing. It can happen with or without them being involved.

2. **Forgiveness does not mean reconciliation.** Forgiveness and reconciliation are two completely different things. You can forgive someone and also choose not to have a relationship with them.

3. **Forgiveness does not mean lack of boundaries.** Even after you forgive, and even if you choose to reconcile, you still have a right to enforce boundaries. Boundaries are like protective fences that say, "You may only come this far in our relationship," or "I will only accept certain types of behavior." Boundaries are necessary for your safety, privacy, and comfortability.

4. **Forgiveness does not mean quickly moving on.** Forgiveness is a journey, and depending on the offense, it may take years to fully heal and forgive. Many times the abused person will have to go through the stages of grief, intense counseling, and a lengthy period of processing. In addition, the forgiveness journey isn't a straight road. Sometimes it is an uphill climb, and it's not uncommon to have both progression and regression during the process.

5. **Forgiveness does not mean excusing or overlooking the wrong.** The abuse was bad, and nothing can be done to change that. Trying to pretend it's all okay is intellectually dishonest and ultimately more damaging.

6. **Forgiveness does not mean forgetting.** I love what Christine Caine says about this: "The blood of Jesus doesn't give you amnesia." Forgiveness doesn't cause you to forget what happened, and that's okay.

7. **Forgiveness does not mean you can't talk about the experience.** This is your story. This is your life. Don't ever let anyone silence or take away your narrative. You can forgive someone and still tell the truth about what happened. Sometimes that is what will bring you the most healing and the best chance of forgiveness.

8. **Forgiveness does not mean there will not be consequences.** Trust is not required to forgive. If someone has broken your trust, only you get to decide if it is safe to rebuild that trust. If someone is abusive, they should expect to experience the consequences for their actions, such as loss of trust, exposure for their wrongdoing, legal action, job loss, relational repercussions, etc.

9. **Forgiveness does not mean you stop keeping track of toxic patterns.** Some abusers will guilt you for keeping track of their repetitive abusive behavior, expecting that your forgiveness will erase past faults and give them a clean slate. That is not the way it works. You can both forgive and document patterns of abuse. Doing so will help you to make safe choices for yourself.

10. **Forgiveness does not mean you should not warn others.** If the abuser is in a position to hurt others, forgiveness doesn't stop you from warning people who need to know about the abusive actions. In some cases it is actually your duty to warn others or report to law enforcement.

I wish I had access to this biblical view of forgiveness years earlier. Of course, I don't know if it would have made a difference. Forgiveness is a journey, and it looks different for everyone. But I know that the day I truly forgave, my life changed. I truly give all the honor and glory to God for that life-changing moment because until I told Him I wasn't willing but was willing to be made willing, I was as far from forgiveness as anyone else.

Remember that it's all part of God's plan. "For I know the plans I have for you, declares the LORD, plans for welfare and not for evil, to give you a future and a hope" (Jeremiah 29:11).

It's so easy to look back and wonder why. Why was I brought up in a cult-minded church and taught such an imbalanced view on the Bible and life? Why was I sheltered but not protected? Why did a trusted adult take advantage of my innocence when I was a minor? Why did I experience so many of my firsts with my abuser? Why didn't my church report her to the proper authorities? Why did I go to an unaccredited college and then go right back to the cultlike church and serve there for six years, taking part in pushing people away from God by advocating the church's twisted positions?

We all ask the what-ifs, but I haven't figured out the answers to mine, nor do I think I will. But I do know this—my best friend is my wife. She's beautiful inside and out. She gets me, and every day she takes my breath away. I have two kids I would literally die for, and I am so proud of them. My family is the reason I hate leaving for work in the morning, the motivation to work so hard during the day, and why I have to watch the speed limit coming home. I love my job, and Karlan's words to me my first day were true. I started as a marketing assistant, but I worked for the company and not the paycheck. Ten years later to the day that I left everything familiar and moved across the country to start over, I was promoted to chief marketing officer. My pay increase was the exact salary I thought I would never be able to replace—twenty-four thousand dollars.

If I had to do it all again, knowing that I could be in this life right here, right now, I would . . . over and over and over. Of course, God could have spared me all the pain and still landed me right where I am, but He chose not to, and I am fine with that.

The lowest time in my life was when I lost my job and the girl I loved in the same day. Because of that, I also lost my reputation and lifelong friendships overnight. With my head hung low, I moved across the country to begin a new life. Ten years later, I can look back amazed at the absolute grace of God that allowed that to happen. If I hadn't lost my job, if Megan hadn't poured her heavy heart out to her parents, if her family hadn't spread so many rumors and lies to the point that I hated myself and thought everyone else did too, I never, ever would have left. I was determined to have my own way, but God took my way from me and moved me on.

I believe with all my heart that it was the best decision for everybody, and I hold no hard feelings toward anyone. God's best for me and everyone else was so much better than my best in 2009, and I'm thankful every day for God's gracious plan.

Know that it's never too late. "I will restore to you the years that the swarming locust has eaten" (Joel 2:25).

My journey of healing and forgiveness took twenty years with many twists and turns. I couldn't even begin to heal until I got away from my abusive environment, which took eleven of those twenty years. The majority of my healing and forgiveness didn't happen until the last two of those twenty years. I am not the same man I was ten years ago, or even six months ago. I have changed in ways I never even thought were possible.

You might have been on your journey for two years or for forty years, and your journey probably looks completely different from mine. Just know that God is faithful and if you let Him, He will change you to where He wants you to be. The outcome might not be what you expected, but it will be His best. It is never, never, never too late to leave your abusive environment, to begin healing, or to make that choice to forgive.

Just take the first step. "The steps of a man are established by the LORD" (Psalm 37:23).

Today, there is not one person in my past that I have any ill will toward. I would break bread with most anyone I've mentioned in this book. That was not true until recently. If forgiveness or healing seems far out of reach and just the thought of it overwhelms you, take the first step, whatever that might be. You don't have to know what the next five steps are, just that next step.

I don't know what that step is for you. Maybe it's to get counseling, or to get as far from your abusive environment as possible. Maybe you've taken all those steps, and forgiveness still isn't an option for you. That's where I was with my abuser halfway through writing this book. It wasn't until I prayed for God to make me willing to be willing to forgive Carol Lynn that I was able to forgive. Wherever you are, just take the first step.

Seek truth. "And you will know the truth, and the truth will set you free" (John 8:32).

For thirty years, I was stuck in a cult-minded church that mixed a little truth with a lot of error. When I left that church at age twenty-nine, I knew something was off about it, but I couldn't articulate what it was. For six years Emily and I discussed our past but felt trapped as to how to change the future. We always concluded, "We may not know how to _____ [raise kids, treat people, find a good church, etc.], but we know how not to, and that's a great first step." It wasn't until we began attending a church that sought to teach truth that we were able to identify exactly what was wrong in the past and establish a plan to change the future for the sake of our family.

The more you know the truth, the easier it will be to detect error. The most skilled carpenters use levels and tape measures to ensure accuracy. Bank tellers handle so much real money throughout the day that they can usually detect counterfeit bills. I am unashamedly a Christian, a Christ follower, and I believe God is truth. He is the benchmark I measure everything against. The more I get to know God, the more glaring counterfeit Christianity becomes. Seek truth!

Writing this book has been a long, hard, fruitful journey, and one I would take again anytime. It has helped me heal. It has brought me closer to my God, my wife, and my kids. It has pulled me further away from toxic friends and family members. It has helped put in perspective my childhood and the good that came out of it. In my efforts to write from a balanced perspective, I have been forced to see the good in bad situations, as well as the bad in seemingly good situations.

Writing this book has changed my life, and I hope reading it changes yours.

Made in the USA
Monee, IL
26 August 2022

12636245R00090